ARABIAN DAYS

ARABIAN DAYS

Tom G. Temperley

The Book Guild Ltd
Sussex, England

The Book Guild Ltd.
25 High Street,
Lewes, Sussex

First published 1994
© Tom G. Temperley
Set in Times
Typesetting by Southern Reproductions (Sussex)
East Grinstead, Sussex
Printed in Great Britain by
Antony Rowe Ltd
Chippenham, Wiltshire.

A catalogue record for this book is
available from the British Library

ISBN 0 86332 956 X

CONTENTS

1

The Beginning

The hot sunlight brushed across my closed eyelids, awakening me with a start to wonder where I was. The muted roar of the four engines of the BOAC Argonaut that had lulled me to sleep during the long night had now hushed to a low rumbling murmur. The public address system broke into life and the captain's voice informed us that we had commenced our descent. We would land in Kuwait within half an hour. The eighteen hour flight from London to Kuwait would be over.

At this signal, the interior of the plane burst into life. Hostesses and stewards appeared bearing hot towels and orange juice. Passengers, who had been lying comatose since boarding the plane in Baghdad, the last refuelling stop, stirred. They removed eye covers and blankets, moving as one for the toilets.

Glancing out of the plane window, I saw we were flying over an area of brilliantly blue water, splashed with patches of bright green shallows, through which the sandy bottom of the sea could plainly be seen.

Random, milky white patches on the surface of the sea caught one's eye. I was to learn that this phenomena, known locally as 'Flashes', indicated areas where there was a sudden precipitation of calcium carbonate from the highly concentrated waters of the Arabian Gulf. Triggered by some curious combination of temperature and concentration in the presence of minute crystals of calcium carbonate, the mechanism is scarcely understood even today. Then, in 1953, it was simply another mystery of the East!

Away in the distant haze, a sandy coastline could be seen stretching away in uninterrupted grandeur. Beyond the coastline, stretching to the horizon was a barren, ochre-coloured, desert terrain; completely devoid of any indication of human habitation. 'What terrible place is this that I have committed myself to for three years,' I thought. 'Surely, by now, there should be some sign of Kuwait City or at least some roads or signs of habitation?'

Shortly, we were sweeping low over a desert landscape for our final approach to Kuwait Airport, the landscape was devoid of any sign of life. It flashed past the plane windows as we neared touch down; a blur of khaki-coloured sand and gravel.

The plane landed with a slight bump and rumbled to a stop in a cloud of fine dust. It turned and taxied bumpily along a rough sand runway, finally coming to rest close to the airport terminal building. This was a single storey, sand-coloured structure of cement blocks, which merged harmoniously with its surroundings. This building, together with a khaki-coloured tent, shimmering in the heat haze rising from the hot ground, were the first signs of human habitation we had seen.

Around the airport in all directions stretched the desert, an unromantic, uninviting, dusty plain, shimmering in the brilliant early morning sunshine.

The engines rumbled to a stop and the plane door

swung open. A blast of furnace-like heat washed into the cool air-conditioned cabin that had been our cocoon for the past eighteen hours. The heat struck our unprepared faces like a physical blow and perspiration already began to prickle my skin beneath my shirt. It was 6.00 a.m. on the morning of June 4th 1953. 'My God!' I thought. 'What sort of place have I come to?'

Three days previously, I had been a power station chemical engineer employed by the then North Western Division of the British Electricity Authority. During the four years that I had been in their employ, I had worked at a number of their power stations in Manchester and Wigan. It was a pleasant and interesting life with the Authority, but wages were low and I could see few prospects in the way of career development other than waiting for the retirement or premature demise of my superiors.

The situation was brought to a head when my motorcycle skidded on an oily patch at a bus stop. Fortunately, I was unhurt but the motorcycle was badly damaged. The bike was only covered by third party insurance, all I could afford at the time. Consequently, there was absolutely no way that I could find the few hundred pounds needed to make it road-worthy once again. There was nothing to do, other than sell the bike for scrap. If I were to become mobile once again other than by means of a push bike, something drastic had to be done!

By chance, I had recently seen two overseas jobs advertised. One was located in Nigeria and the other in the Sheikhdom of Kuwait. The Nigerian job offered the salary of twelve hundred pounds sterling per annum, while the Kuwait post offered slightly more, fifteen hundred pounds per year! In comparison to my current salary of seven pounds per week these were princely sums indeed. I reasoned that on such salaries, I would be able to save sufficient cash to purchase a new motor bike; perhaps even a new car. With this tempting thought in mind, I decided to apply for both positions.

To my great surprise and considerable gratification, I was offered both jobs. My final selection between the two posts was based solely upon the greed of gold! I must confess, I gave no thought to the long term future, or to the development of a career. Fifteen hundred pounds sounded so much better than twelve hundred. Kuwait won the day.

I had read much literature, both fact and fiction, concerning Africa and Nigeria. They had many attractions for a young man, but I knew absolutely nothing about Kuwait. In fact, until I went for my interview, I was not aware where in the world Kuwait was located, or that it was ruled by a benevolent and enlightened despot, Sheikh Sir Abdullah Salim Al-Subah.

The position offered in Kuwait was that of Chief Chemist and Chemical Engineer with the Department of Electricity. I was led to understand by the job description that my duties would be involved in chemical and corrosion control of the various aspects of power generation and sea water desalination, both areas of which I had some knowledge through my current work with the Electricity Authority.

The letter of appointment informed me that the Chief Engineer of the Kuwait Government's Department of Electricity, a Mr J. D. Addison, required my presence in Kuwait immediately. Consequently, within two months of applying for the post and some three days after leaving the Electricity Authority, I was sitting in a British Overseas Airways Argonaut aeroplane *en route* for Kuwait International Airport, experiencing the blistering heat of a Kuwait summer morning for the first time in my life. Little did I know that I was about to disembark into a new life and career that were to cover the next forty years.

Prior to obtaining the post, I had attended an interview in London at the offices of Ewbank & Partners, a prestigious firm of consulting engineers. Here I was subjected to detailed, probing questions by a series of imposing, elderly gentlemen uniformly garbed in pinstripe trousers and dark coats. Their stiff white collars were relieved by ties in the distinctive colours of various professional institutes. Their grave judicial appearance and the probing nature of their questions soon had me in an acute state of nerves. Fortunately, the growing stress of the interview was relieved by a disturbance outside the office.

The solemn, almost church-like atmosphere that pervaded the offices and interview room was suddenly disrupted. A large, heavy-jowled gentleman carrying an umbrella and bowler hat entered the building. In a loud imperative bellow, he enquired with forceful authority as to who the devil had the temerity to park their car in the slot specifically reserved for his Rolls Royce?

Immediately, the whole office erupted in panic. Even the two elderly gentlemen conducting my interview hurriedly left the room to join other members of the staff encircling and attempting to placate the irate gentleman, who was later identified to me as Mr Harry Ewbank, the senior partner of the firm.

Immediate action was taken to correct the matter. The staff rushed out into the street to remove the offending vehicle by pushing it into a 'No Parking Zone' across the street. The Rolls was then established

11

in its rightful place, immediately outside the main entrance to the office.

When my interviewers rejoined me some fifteen minutes later, I had been able to calm my over-stretched nerves to some degree. They, on the other hand, had been badly shaken by the violent tantrum of their principal partner who had castigated all in sight for allowing someone to usurp his personal parking spot. As a consequence, my interviewers appeared to have lost heart in their task and the interview degenerated into a friendly, informal chat. They described life in Kuwait as they knew it and referenced the various people I would meet, should I be appointed to the post.

As they had only visited Kuwait at random intervals for a few days at a time their knowledge of the place was flimsy to say the least. Consequently, they provided me with a completely inaccurate picture of local conditions and the description of the job I was supposed to fill. When I finally left their office, it was with a totally false idea of life in Kuwait at that time.

A week later I received a formal offer of employment directly from the Department of Electricity in Kuwait, together with an air ticket and a request to proceed as quickly as possible to Kuwait to take up my new post. Hectic preparations started immediately. I underwent a comprehensive medical examination. A passport was obtained with the necessary visa. A seat was booked on the earliest flight to Kuwait and a first class seat reserved on the train from Manchester to Euston station, London.

Suitable tropical clothing was purchased upon the advice of an authoritative, bespoke tailor of tropical clothing. My final outfit (purchased at great personal expense I may add), included heavy shirts fitted with spin pads to protect me from the tropical heat, knee length shorts and long white stockings to protect my legs from the sun's rays and a cork topee, complete with neck shield to protect me from sun stroke.

Upon arriving in Kuwait, I was to find that all this protective gear was completely redundant. With few exceptions, most people went bareheaded, wore thin cotton shirts, extremely short cotton shorts with bare legs and Arabic style, open-toed, leather sandals.

My attention was once again focused upon the present. The door of the plane was opened wider and the in-rushing desert air was like the discharge from a blast furnace. In my work in the power industry I had experienced similar temperatures on the tops of high pressure boiler plant, but never had imagined that such temperatures existed in nature.

The captain's voice announced that the Kuwaiti authorities had now given permission for the passengers to disembark and upon the steward's directive, we moved forward to file through the door and down the steps onto the sun-baked ground. It was only then, as the intense dry heat flowed over us, that I realized the significance of the fact that it was still only 6.00 a.m. in the morning. If the incredible heat of the Kuwait summer was already in evidence, what would it be like at noon?

Under the watchful eye of a somewhat disreputable-looking armed guard dressed in dingy khaki drill and a red and white check Arab style headdress carrying a shabby-looking rifle, we disembarked and walked the few yards to the single storey building. Here we presented our passports for inspection to a waiting official. Standing at a battered wooden desk directly under a whirring ceiling fan, he stamped and returned them to us. Immigration formalities completed, we moved over to a low trestle table to collect our baggage and clear customs.

Throughout the journey I had sat next to a lady with a young baby in a carrycot. She informed me that her husband was an engineer with the Department of Electricity with whom I would work. The Peacocks, as they were called, lived in a small villa in a government housing area called Sulaibikhat.

Each time we had disembarked from the plane at the various refuelling stops during the trip, Frankfurt, Rome, Beirut and Baghdad, I had been of assistance in carrying her hand baggage from the plane to the terminal. The weight of the baggage, particularly the baby's carrycot was surprising. When I remarked upon the weight, she informed me that the baby's carrycot and her hand baggage was full of soil that she had taken from her garden in England. It was intended for bedding house plants that she was trying to grow at her home in Kuwait.

She told me that the saline soil of Kuwait was unsuitable for growing anything but hardy desert plants. In an attempt to compensate for the barren nature of their surroundings the European residents made heroic efforts to cultivate indoor plants. This was carried to such a point that many houses had the appearance and atmosphere of tropical greenhouses! Mrs Peacock was typical of the plant growing expatriate residents of Kuwait. It was apparently quite common practice for the expatriates to bring soil, compost and seeds back whenever they returned from leave. The other expats waited with baited breath to see what new species of plants their returning colleagues had brought with them; hopeful of obtaining cuttings or a few spare seeds for their own cultivation.

14

The layer of sweet earth in the baby's carrycot and a similar layer in her hand baggage seemed not to surprise the customs official at all. Perhaps today, after the introduction of the vampire movies and a wider knowledge of the need for these creatures to carry around samples of the earth from their homeland, he might well have had some misgivings. At that time the significance was lost on him and he marked the bags without comment.

After clearing customs, we moved from the building, past a further uniformed and armed guard, to join a small group of Europeans awaiting our arrival.

Two people approached us. One a tall man of about my own age, obviously the lady's husband, introduced himself as John Peacock, a charge engineer at the station. The second person was an elderly, short, tubby gentleman in an open necked shirt and grey flannel slacks. He introduced himself as Pop Demain, the Superintendent of the power and desalination plant at Shuwaikh and my immediate superior. He explained that he had come to welcome me to Kuwait and take me to my new accommodation.

My baggage was loaded into his car, a large, metallic grey, Humber 'Super Snipe' saloon parked in the airport car park, by one of the many Iranian porters eagerly seeking the opportunity to be of service for a few rupees. We climbed into the furnace-like interior of the car, where the hot seats made sitting anything but comfortable.

Mr Demain started the engine and we drove along a dirt road towards the city. The road crossed the open desert for two of three miles before approaching a fortified gate set in a high adobe mud wall. The gateway, the fortified wall around the city, the buildings and road were all the same dusty sand colour. It was not at all surprising that I had not been able to see any structures from the air. The wall, fortifications and buildings, I was to learn, were made from a mixture of dead coral, sand and 'gatch', a calcium sulphate rich clay, which sets like concrete in the heat of the sun.

We drove through the gateway, which I later learned was called Naif Gate, and entered the City of Kuwait proper. On either side of the roadway single storey buildings, constructed in the same material as the fortified wall, contained open fronted shops and workshops. They offered vehicle spare parts, services and a variety of merchandise that was not easily recognized from the interior of the car.

Pop Demain threaded his way skilfully through a variety of traffic including two-wheeled carts drawn by emaciated horses, rickety taxis (mainly Ford Pilot saloon cars) of considerable vintage and balloon tyred Humber Snipe pickups (the standard Kuwait Oil Company vehicles, which were modified especially for desert work I was to learn).

There were also large numbers of camels, all loaded high with huge packs wrapped in multi-coloured blankets. Their drovers, seated high above the other traffic on the road, guided their mounts with nonchalant flicks of their camel goads, uttering sharp guttural cries of *'Haht, haht!'* to encourage their beasts to move more quickly through the hodge podge of traffic, clouds of dust and blaring horns. The noise and colour provided me with my first real sense of Arabia.

Pop drove unhurriedly along the dirt road, skilfully avoiding potholes and the continuous flow of people, animals and vehicles crossing his path. All appeared to be completely oblivious to other traffic on the road, or the people around them.

Eventually, after a number of hair raising near misses with a camel and an Iranian porter staggering along with a huge refrigerator on his back, we arrived at a large open area in the centre of Kuwait City. Pop explained that this was Safat Square, the centre of Kuwait City. Various government offices and banks were located along the eastern side of the Safat. On the northern side of the square was New Street or the Street of Pillars as it was known. Bebehani and Jashenmal's stores, the main departmental stores at that time, were also located to the north of the square.

We parked the car and made our way through a milling international throng of Kuwaitis, Gulf Arabs, Palestinians, Egyptians, Pakistanis, Indians and Europeans, all hurrying about their business, intent only upon their own affairs. I could have stood and watched the colourful crowd all day. Pop, however, had other priorities and hurried me onwards.

Crossing Safat Square, we entered the British Bank of The Middle East, a large sand-coloured building. Large groups of people crowded and jostled around service points at the counter. Confusion was the order of the day! The orderly lines of customers waiting to be served, that one would expect in a British bank, were non-existent. Everyone pushed and jostled each other, all attempting to reach a vantage point against the counter, from which they could attract the attention of the clerk.

The majority held an arm aloft in the air, waving a cheque, letter or document like a signal flag. Anything that might be used to attract the attention of the clerk was brandished vigorously, in the forlorn hope that he would take pity and select them particularly from the clamouring multitude. The service clerk studiously ignored all their

17

blandishments and went on with his work, completely oblivious to the efforts being made to gain his attention.

Without hesitation, like a ship under full sail, Pop moved resolutely into one of the groups milling around a counter clerk. Elbowing people to right and left, he rapidly pushed to the front of the group, towing me somewhat apologetically behind him. To my considerable surprise, no-one appeared to object to this cavalier treatment. By means of some hypnotic power, Pop captured the attention of the clerk behind the counter. He immediately ceased whatever he was doing and moved to open a small door, allowing us access into the area behind the counter.

Pop went directly to a desk at which a rather harassed-looking European was sitting behind a pile of files and documents, which he studiously read one by one, before endorsing and consigning them to a further pile of documents. These were periodically removed and carried to another desk by one of the many messengers who moved between the various desks. He was continuously being interrupted by *farashes,* office messengers, carrying documents and files which were being added to the already large piles upon his desk.

Pop introduced us. We sat in two chairs at the side of the desk while he continued to work as we chatted. Sweet mint tea was served to us in small glass cups by a rather grubby-looking tea boy. This was immediately followed by a cold fizzy orange drink known locally as *sinalco.*

The niceties of local protocol being observed, we turned to the business of the day – namely, I discovered, to open a bank account for me. The relevant formalities were completed speedily and within a remarkably short time I was handed a new cheque book, and an invitation to a cocktail party to be held at the house of the bank manager later in the week.

As we left the bank, Pop drew my attention to a number of metallic bars in open wooden boxes lying scattered around the bank floor. A closer inspection revealed these to be gold ingots! People were stepping over and around them completely ignoring the fortune lying at their feet. Pop told me that there was virtually no crime in Kuwait, consequently, it was hardly necessary to take the precautions against theft that would have been essential in Europe. A combination of extremely severe penalties, together with the strict code of living taught by the Muslim religion appeared to be sufficient to control the incidence of local crime. I later learned that this incidence of low crime rates also applied to the other Gulf States and Saudi Arabia.

Our next port of call was the Finance Department. This was located in a bare and austere-looking building, some fifty metres from the bank. Here were housed the various financial departments of the Government. At that time, control of all the expenditure of the Kuwaiti Government was carried out within its walls.

A mass of people, the majority carrying large sheaves of paper, milled around an open courtyard within the centre of the building, overflowing through dingy interconnecting corridors and dark stairways. No-one appeared to be quite sure where they were going in this maze of dim corridors and anonymous, unmarked, closed doors. Everyone that is, except Pop Demain. Without slackening his pace, Pop strode through the crowd; scattering people to left and right. Following closely in his wake, I mounted a flight of dingy, tile stairs leading to an upper corridor. Pop made a swift right turn and entered a small office furnished with a desk and chair and a dusty looking three piece suite that appeared to have seen better days.

Here I was introduced to Mrs Loise Rothwell, the secretary. She was sitting at the wooden desk, behind a large pile of dusty files. I was to learn later that Loise was the wife of Bill Rothwell, the Chief Surgeon in the Department of Health. Like many other expatriate wives, in order to pass the time, she worked part-time as a departmental secretary in one of the various government offices.

The majority of households employed at least one servant. Consequently, there was little to occupy the time of the expatriate wives. They passed their days entertaining friends at coffee mornings, taking part-time jobs with the governmental departments, or doing voluntary work in the hospitals and clinics. A number of wives taught at the Shuwaikh School, a small school organized by the British community for expatriate children.

With Loise's permission we passed into an inner office, slightly better furnished than the outer room, and with the added prestige of a dusty carpet on the floor! Four expatriates sat around a desk chatting and drinking coffee. They stood as we entered. Pop introduced George Strover, whose office it was, Colin McGregor, Paul Pocock and Bill Duff.

The head of the department was currently on leave and George Strover as his deputy was in charge. Paul Pocock was the accountant responsible for the financial management of the Department of Electricity and worked closely with Pop Demain. Colin McGregor and Bill Duff were involved in the control of incoming funds from the oil revenues.

After a few minutes' informal chat and a further glass

of sweet mint tea, I was given a contract to read and sign. The ceremony was sealed with another glass of tea. With my copy of the contract in one pocket and my cheque book in the other, we left the cool shade of the Finance Department to once again brave the Kuwait morning sun. It was now almost noon and the heat and intense glare of the sunlight reflecting from the light-coloured ground was almost unbearable.

Our next port of call was the Shuwaikh Bachelor Camp, a group of single storey, barrack-like buildings where I was to be housed until I moved into more salubrious permanent quarters. At the camp I was introduced to Mr Angus McDonald, the manager of the Shuwaikh Housing Department and his assistant, Mr Tuite-Dalton.

Angus was a heavily built imposing figure, obviously enjoying the authority and influence his position gave him. Prior to joining the Government Housing Department, Angus had worked in the personnel section of the Kuwait Oil Company where he was affectionately known as 'Angus McTravel'. Apparently, he had left the Kuwait Oil Company's employ shortly after he had arranged passages for a couple of British engineers on a tanker bound for Newcastle. Not surprisingly, they were upset and complained bitterly to the company when they found that the first land fall was to be Newcastle, Australia! Angus's wife, Dolly, was also an employee of the Government. She ran the Government Guest House where official guests and VIP visitors were entertained.

Tuite-Dalton was a mild, rather shy man, completely overshadowed by Angus. He sat quietly mopping his face with a large handkerchief while Angus pontificated upon the strict regulations governing the residents of the camp. It was the responsibility of

Tuite-Dalton to see that Angus's instructions and policies were implemented.

I was to learn that an intense rivalry existed between Angus and the camp residents who disliked him intensely. The residents were mainly contractors' employees who resented the attempts of Angus and his staff to restrict their activities. As some of their wilder social activities had included jousting tournaments using jeeps and scaffolding poles, shooting up the mess with · 22 rifles (one man being shot in the leg during this particular episode), flooding the club piano with beer and setting fire to toilet rolls wound around the ceiling fans in the mess, Angus's attempts to limit their excesses was understandable. The residents, on the other hand, regarded Angus and his staff as interfering busy-bodies.

I was finally directed to my accommodation, room A in block 8. The accommodation comprised a small, sparsely furnished bed-sitter containing a single bed, a desk, two easy chairs, a hardback chair and a wardrobe. The room was cooled by means of a noisy air conditioning unit set in the wall opposite the bed. The air conditioner was effective, but was prone to make alarming bangs and clattering noises as the compressor came into service. After the intense heat outdoors, the room was deliciously cool and restful.

Pop said that he would now leave me to my own devices for the afternoon, but would collect me in the evening to take me to a reception to be held in my honour at the home of the Chief Engineer, Mr J. D. Addison. The intention was to introduce me to the senior staff of the Electricity Department, as well as to various leading figures in the local expatriate community.

When Pop departed, an Indian houseboy smartly

22

dressed in white shirt and trousers entered. He introduced himself as John, the houseboy assigned to my room. John unpacked my belongings, stowing them carefully away in the drawers and wardrobe. He informed me that his duties included looking after my laundry, cleaning my room and general domestic requirements. Although John looked little older than fifteen or sixteen, I learned with surprise that back in Goa, his home state in India, he had a wife and two teenage children! So much for appearances.

I was later to learn that John's great weakness was alcohol. Apparently, he tapped the liquor stocks of each of his sahibs while cleaning their rooms. Consequently, as he looked after some ten expatriates, John would float through the day in a haze of alcohol. To his credit, this never interfered with his work or affected his disposition which was always cheerful. He was fiercely loyal to all his sahibs, and guarded their interests with intense devotion.

After unpacking my things, John directed me to the mess hall where I could obtain lunch. He also gave detailed instructions how to obtain a liquor licence in order to purchase a stock of liquor for my room. Unfortunately for John and his refreshment programme, I was a keep-fit enthusiast, and did not drink. Later I found it to be necessary to carry a stock of liquor for social hospitality, thus after all, becoming one of John's unknowing benefactors.

The mess hall was located in the centre of the camp complex. The menu was changed daily and the food was excellent. The method of payment was by ticket. Books of different value tickets were on sale at a desk at the entrance to the mess. These tickets could be exchanged for selections from the menu of the day. To complicate matters, change was always given in the form of loose tickets. Consequently, after some time one accumulated a number of partially empty books and a mass of loose tickets, a large proportion of which were lost or torn beyond redemption.

After buying a book of tickets from the cashier, I entered the mess hall and took a seat at a vacant table. It was unbelievably hot, for some reason the mess hall was not air conditioned. The room was cooled by large ceiling fans which rotated at high speed with a loud rushing noise. They provided a continuous stream of hot air, blowing table cloths and napkins about as if in a gale.

The waiters, dressed in white shirts and trousers with black cummerbunds and matching bow ties, stood around the walls of the hall. They watched the diners with eagle eyes, ready to pounce at the first indication that their services might be required. I enjoyed my lunch in the unusual surroundings and heat. After paying from my book of tickets, I returned to the cool of my room and cast myself on the bed luxuriating in the cold draught from the air conditioner. Almost immediately I fell into a deep, dreamless sleep.

John, the room boy, woke me at 4.30 p.m. with a cup of tea. I showered and decided to familiarize myself with the camp and its various amenities. I stepped out of my room into the heat of the late afternoon. Although still extremely hot, the biting heat and brilliance of the noontime sun was gone. The air was still hot to the skin, but the humidity was low and it was quite pleasant to walk around in the open air.

The camp was composed of a number of single storey residence blocks set within a fenced area of barren ground. Each block comprised a number of rooms. They were similar in all respects to my room in block 8. All opened onto a common corridor with communal showers, toilets and a refrigerator room. The camp amenities comprised the mess hall, an open air cinema, a social club and a bar. In addition, there were tennis courts and a billiard room.

I later discovered that the 'Film Nights' on Tuesday and Friday, together with the weekly dance on Thursday evening, were the main social events of the week. All the expatriate community religiously attended these evenings which were regarded as social occasions where friends could meet and forget the heat, the flies and problems of the day.

On film evenings, the quality and subject of the films were considered to be secondary to the opportunity to meet and chat with friends. Prior to the film and during the three intervals while the reels were changed, viewers met and chatted in small groups, arranging their social calendars and planning their weekend activities. Later, after the film show, it was common practice for the residents of the camp to invite their various friends back to their rooms for tea or coffee and biscuits. Groups would crowd into the tiny rooms chatting, gossiping and drinking large volumes of tea late into the evening.

One particular camp resident, John Shipton, was an extremely talented musician. John also held 'Open House' after the cinema, plying his friends with tea and biscuits as did other residents of the camp. In addition, John would play his Hammond organ for their pleasure. It was a great privilege to be invited to John Shipton's room for tea after the film show.

John also provided the music for the weekly dances held at the club. Initially, he organized a dance band from the camp residents able to play an instrument. As members of his band left or lost interest, he decided that it was less complicated to rely upon his own talents. He played dance music on the organ with an electronic 'sideman' providing the rhythm section.

'Shippy', as he was affectionately known, played the organ (his second instrument) at the local American Mission Church. Rain or shine, he played for the Sunday services, expatriate or Christian weddings and sadly now and then, at the odd funeral. John also had a third Hammond organ, this was left at the local Masonic Temple where John provided harmony on lodge nights.

'Shippy' was an extremely kind and gifted person, giving unstintingly of his time to the annual pantomime and other musical shows produced by the local theatrical groups. Being so talented himself, he was somewhat intolerant of less gifted persons. During pantomime rehearsals he complained bitterly to anyone who would listen, that although he played the black notes and the white notes, the vocalists insisted upon singing in the cracks between them!'

The Camp Social Club was a single storey concrete block building containing a bar, a dance floor and billiard room with a full size table and facilities for table tennis and darts. Adjacent to the Club were two hard surface tennis courts which were in great demand during the winter months. A weekly dance was held each Thursday from 7.00 p.m., lasting into the early hours of Friday morning. Tombola was also extremely popular, being played twice per week.

The bar, open daily at lunch time and again in the evenings, was a focus of activity for many expatriates. In addition to the casual social drinkers who called in for a drink before a meal or the cinema, a hard core of regulars could always be found there. These tended to be the 'characters' of the expatriate community. This group included a number of strange, flamboyant people, interesting to meet, but unwise to cultivate too closely. Unless, of course, one wished to be drawn into their complicated world of too much drink, unpaid debts and family troubles.

Darkness fell suddenly without the usual twilight of the British summer evening. With the darkness came an oppressive humidity, which sent me hurrying back to the cool of my room to shower and await the arrival of Pop Demain, who would take me to the reception and cocktail party at the Addison's home.

Pop arrived on schedule, and we departed for our host's house located in the senior staff residential area in north Shuwaikh. Some wag had named the district 'Champagne Row'. The name stuck. Even the residents used this descriptive title for the district.

The houses were large Spanish style villas built in stucco coated breeze block. As the majority of the residents could either afford the services of a gardener or were able to use their department's labour, the houses had large well tended gardens. The presence of a green lawn or a bed of flowers in this arid land lent added charm to the house and provided a status symbol for the tenant.

Jim Addison and his charming wide, Maidie, proved to be most congenial hosts. They spared no effort to make me feel at home. At least until Jim Addison casually informed me that there were two groups of people that he did not trust, namely, architects and chemists. He said that he regarded both professions as 'evil necessities'! As my father was an architect and I was a chemist and chemical engineer, it appeared that I was a two time loser!

Suddenly, my future with the Kuwaiti Government did not appear as rosy as I had first thought. Fortunately, Jim Addison's bark was far worse than his bite. Over the ensuing years, I believe we developed considerable respect for each other. Jim Addison had been in private business in India before joining the Kuwait Oil Company as their chief engineer. Later, at the request of the ruler, he had transferred to the Department of Electricity in Kuwait under Sheikh Jabir Al Ali.

Jim Addison, or JDA, as he was known to his staff, was an Abadonian by birth. He displayed all the characteristic frugality associated with the natives of that part of Scotland, much to the discomfort of his employees when salaries were under consideration. A capable engineer, he was a hard task master, who demanded maximum effort and dedication from all his staff.

Many of his staff disliked him intensely, a few liked him, but all respected him, conceding perhaps grudgingly, that he was a first class engineering manager. On the other hand, Mrs Addison was popular and well liked by all. She was always able to heal the rifts that her husband's abrasive manner provoked.

The Addisons took me round and introduced me to their guests, setting me at ease by their hospitable and friendly attitude. In addition to the various government departmental heads, they had thoughtfully invited a number of power and desalination plant personnel. I was particularly pleased to talk to them, and obtain as much background information as possible with regard to the plant and my new job.

It was while Jim Addison was introducing me to this latter group that a thin, sharp-faced, middle-aged lady stepped forward, confronting JDA.

'When are you going to give my husband the increase in salary he deserves?' she said in a loud Irish accent. Conversation in the room died and all eyes turned towards the lady and Jim Addison. He never hesitated.

'Ah yes! I am looking into it, ask your husband to come into the office to see me tomorrow morning,' he said. 'The office is a much better place to discuss such matters.' After a few pleasantries he moved off as though nothing had occurred.

The lady's husband looked as though he wished the floor would open and swallow him. I don't believe that JDA ever held the incident against him, but he never received the increase. Jim Addison rarely gave increases during a contract!

The evening passed pleasantly. Everyone went out of their way to make me welcome. I was inundated with invitations to dinner, curry lunches, beach parties, Scottish dancing, amateur dramatics etc. Towards the end of the evening Pop Demain approached me to say that Mr Addison had asked him to remain behind to discuss business. He had therefore requested his son-in-law, Len Griffiths, the desalination plant Maintenance Engineer to drive me home.

Len Griffiths and Margaret, his wife, were a pleasant couple near my own age. Len kindly offered to collect me on the following morning to take me into work. As he explained, until I could arrange to obtain my own car, I would be dependent upon others for transport, it was too hot to walk any distance in the heat of the Kuwaiti summer.

My room was deliciously cool after the heat and humidity of the outdoors. A quick shower and I was soon in bed in a dreamless sleep.

The room boy woke me the following morning at 4.30 a.m. with a pot of tea and some toast, and I was up and dressed when Len Griffiths arrived shortly afterwards to take me to work.

At the desalination plant, Len quickly showed me around, introducing me to the various personnel on duty. After the guided tour of the facility, Len left me in the laboratory where my assistant, and later good friend, Arthur Tauro B.Sc., an Indian national from Madras, familiarized me with the daily routine. Arthur introduced me to the other members of my staff. These included:

Haji Khambar, a fiery little Persian Shiite Moslem. A fanatic with regard to his religious beliefs, Haji would beat himself with chains during the month of Muharam until he bled, requiring hospital treatment. Haji was not alone in his religious flagellation. Throughout the Gulf States and Iran similar devotees to the Shiite faith beat and cut themselves during the period of penitence.

Haji was our Chemical Treatment Operator. He, under the direction of a chemist, weighed and added the daily chemical dosages to the various chemical treatment tanks. In addition, Haji cleaned the laboratory and made tea for the staff and visitors. He prided himself that everyone in the laboratory had a hot glass of strong, milky tea to hand at all times and was deeply offended should anyone refuse. He was never satisfied until they finally accepted a cup from him.

Khadam Shah was the foreman of the chemical cleaning team. A large, muscular Patan from the North West Frontier, he was headman of his tribe and a man to be reckoned with. He was a fiercely loyal, hardworking member of the staff. From time to time he was called home to Patan to redress some point of honour on behalf of his tribe. Usually, this meant that he had to kill a member of a rival tribe across the valley. On a number of occasions Khadam Shah's return from leave was delayed because he had been wounded in a shooting affray. Sadly, circumstances finally caught up with him and he was mortally wounded. It was with great sadness that we learned that he had been killed and would not be returning to lead his chemical cleaning team into the fray against the boiler and evaporator scale deposits.

Abbas Salim Shatti was a Kuwaiti national in charge of the chemical treatment activities on the plant. He was extremely hardworking by any standard. Over the years he was to become my close friend and later, a business partner.

These people, together with a number of assistant chemists, engineers, tradesmen and helpers comprised the staff in the chemical engineering and laboratory department, where I was to work for the ensuing seventeen years.

The work proved to be extremely interesting and I soon developed my own routines and procedures. My responsibilities involved the control of day to day plant operations as well as carrying out experiments with a view to improving performance and increasing efficiency of the desalination process. In addition to the general plant work, we were also responsible for the chemical and corrosion control work associated with all government facilities. These included all the electro-mechanical services for the hospitals, schools, waste treatment plants, power stations, swimming pools, government buildings, pumping stations etc. through-out the State of Kuwait.

This varied work brought me into contact with a large number of Kuwaitis as well as the expatriate population. Many of the latter were larger than life characters, the like of whom I had never met before, or for that matter, since.

31

I soon fell into the Kuwaiti routine of work and leisure. The early start to the eight hour day, 5.30 a.m. to 1.30 p.m., allowed adequate free time. After lunch, one took an afternoon siesta during the heat of the day. Subsequently, after being wakened by the houseboy with a cup of tea and a biscuit, it was common practice to go to the beach for a swim before dinner. After eating, there was either the cinema, tombola in the Club, or the weekend dance. Alternatively, there could be an invitation to someone's house for the evening.

It soon became apparent that some means of personal transport was essential. Paul Pocock, the Ministry of Finance representative at the plant, was of invaluable assistance to me in obtaining a driving licence. I had never driven a car before, but I did have a provisional motorcycle licence. On the strength of this Paul was able to obtain a full driving licence for me. Within a few days I was the proud possessor of Kuwait Driving Licence No. 196.

Immediately I received the licence, I commenced the process of purchasing a car. Once again, Paul came to my rescue. The Chief Storekeeper at the plant, Abdullah Hussain, one of Paul's staff, was assigned to me with the specific brief to obtain a car for me as quickly as possible.

Abdullah, a slightly built, middle-aged Palestinian with the most complete set of gold teeth that I have ever seen, was also one of the nicest and kindest people I have had the pleasure of meeting. Nothing was too much trouble for him. Each afternoon at 4.00 p.m., he would collect me in a battered grey Morris Minor saloon. He would drive from showroom to showroom without complaint. We examined car after car from luxurious Packards, Chryslers and Cadillacs to the less glamorous Morris Minors and Fords at the lower end of the market.

My purse would not extend to the American cars. Consequently, my final decision rested between a white Ford Zephyr convertible and an MG TF model in British racing green. After considerable heart searching and many changes of mind, I settled upon the MG TF.

The MG agent, Abdullah Mullah, was also *Wazir* to the Ruler, his Prime Minister. His garage and showrooms were managed by a Scottish gentleman by the name of Cyril Cant. Cyril was a Mr Fixit of the first order! He not only ran Abdullah Mullah's garage, but also handled most of Abdullah's engineering business and acted as a general trouble shooter for all his operations as well.

As soon as Cyril received my order for the MG TF, he promised to have the car ready for collection the following afternoon. I had to collect it from the main garage in the eastern part of the city. This meant that I would have to drive the car through the city centre at the busiest time of the day. Not a project that I relished. Still, having Abdullah along gave me confidence and I agreed to collect the car at the appointed time.

I did not tell Abdullah that I had never driven a car before as it did not appear to be wise to shake his confidence in me at this stage of the project! With hindsight though, he may have suspected that I was not a driver. When he called to collect me the following day he was not in his own car. Thoughtfully, he had arranged for a friend to collect us and drive us to the garage. I presume this was in case he might be required to drive the car for me.

When we arrived at the garage, Cyril Cant had the car ready for us. It was a new TF model, resplendent in British racing green. The headlamps were built into the body, a new innovation for British cars. With my previous experience being limited to push bikes and a vintage motorcycle some years older than myself, this was indeed a dream car! Even Abdullah seemed to be suitably impressed when he saw it.

Hurriedly, I signed the acceptance papers and insurance forms, received the keys from Cyril and stepped into my new car.

Abdullah tactfully suggested that as I was still not familiar with Kuwaiti roads, it would be better if I let him drive my car back to the Shuwaikh camp! I would have none of this.

I started the car without difficulty. Applying my theoretical knowledge to the full, I moved the car into first gear and we moved off, in a series of kangaroo-like jumps, towards the garage gate. Fortunately, the gatekeeper was something of an athlete. He managed to beat us to the barrier which he raised just in the nick of time, allowing us to pass beneath it with inches to spare.

My last impression as we passed under the gate was a view of Cyril Cant in the mirror. He was clutching his head with both hands and staring after us with a look of pure anguish on his face.

The way back to the Shuwaikh camp led through the centre of Kuwait City along the route that I had previously travelled with Pop Demain a few days earlier. We progressed steadily homeward in a series of jerks and bunny hops. We threaded and swerved our way amongst the pedestrians, vehicles and camels. All blissfully unaware of the extreme danger they faced as we progressed through the city. In a few near miss situations people leapt out of our way shaking their fists and shouting appropriate oaths in their native tongue.

Abdullah sat frozen in his seat, grasping the passenger handle on the dashboard with both hands, his knuckles gleaming white through the skin. He stared straight ahead, muttering prayers to Allah for our safe deliverance. At intervals of maximum stress (they occurred quite frequently), he broke off to shout 'Oh God! Oh God! Sahib'. In one instance when the nose of the car actually passed beneath the rear bumper of a huge Mercedes truck, he gave vent to a shrill scream, then immediately returned to his prayer, but this time with closed eyes.

Unless one had the actual experience, it would be difficult to imagine the traffic density and the chaos in the narrow unmade streets at that time of day. Even experienced drivers avoided the centre of the city in the early evening. How we ever managed to reach the safety of the Shuwaikh camp without a serious accident I will never know. Possibly Abdullah's fervent prayers helped! However, as the traffic density became thinner and my driving skills improved slightly, the last few miles from the city centre were quite pleasant and I began to enjoy myself.

On the other hand poor Abdullah continued to suffer traumatically until we reached the confines of the camp and I stopped the car. Immediately Abdullah excused himself. He politely declined my offer of a lift home and flagged down a passing taxi; driving off without a backward glance. I suspect that he went directly to attend the *Magreb,* the Muslim evening prayer, to deliver fervent thanks for his safe deliverance.

The following day he told everyone at work, with suitable embellishments, of his 'Death Ride' through the city. His experience proved a great conversation piece in the local coffee shop, ensuring him an endless supply of coffee from his avid and sympathetic listeners who were delighted to hear further confirmation of the madness of the British.

As soon as Abdullah had left, I took the car out again. This time, after an exploratory drive around the camp, I drove to a remote area along the Ahmedi Road. Here I practised starting, reversing, gear changing etc. By the end of the evening I had acquired a reasonable command of the vehicle, and had gained sufficient confidence to drive on the main road without being too great a risk to other road users.

I returned to the camp and immediately washed and polished the vehicle which already had become my pride and joy. Then, exhausted after a long working day and the hours spent in the considerable heat of the Kuwaiti afternoon, I had a cold shower and went straight to bed, too tired to even eat dinner.

2

Kuwait As It Was

The new car immediately extended my social horizons. Previously, I had been dependent upon others to take me to work, into town to shop and to the beach in the afternoons and at weekends. Now I could go as I pleased. My days became full of things to do, and I began to thoroughly enjoy my life in Kuwait.

Because of the intense heat of the Kuwaiti summer, our working day commenced at 5.30 a.m., for a continuous eight hours without a break until 1.30 p.m. We then took a quick lunch before retiring for an afternoon siesta. The afternoon shade temperatures as high as fifty-five degrees centigrade, and sun temperatures in excess of eighty-five degrees centigrade, made it almost impossible to work out of doors during the heat of the day.

Unless one has actually experienced the intense heat of a Kuwaiti summer without the advantages of air conditioned offices and cars, it is difficult to imagine the enervating effect of the intense heat during the day and the moist heat of the humid evenings. During the day, the harsh glare of the sunlight reflected from the sand dazzled the eyes, even when wearing tinted sunglasses. Perspiration continuously ran into one's eyes, causing them to burn and sting with the salt.

The heat and light from the sun, augmented by reflection from the sea, sand and the light colour of the buildings, beat remorselessly upon one's senses like a drum. One could almost hear the sun's rays hammering upon the ground. Objects standing in direct sunlight for even a short period of time, quickly became too hot to touch without burning the hand. The desert breeze in mid-summer was like the draught from an open furnace door and the air was so hot it caught at one's throat and lungs like liquid fire.

The interior of a car standing in the open sunlight, for even a short time, rapidly became unbearably hot. Desert-wise Kuwaitis and expatriates placed a white cloth over the windscreen to deflect some of the heat. Another trick was to fit a material cover or glove around the steering wheel to save burning one's hands and a wicker seat cover to protect their legs from the hot leather or plastic of the seat.

The more knowledgeable and experienced among us would secret a wicker 'cool seat' in the shade under the dash panel. This would escape the direct heat of the sun and remain cool enough to sit upon in relative comfort whenever one returned to the car. Without the use of a 'cool seat' or a thick towel as insulation, it wasn't possible to sit with any degree of comfort upon leather or fabric car seats.

It was a particularly traumatic experience for the unwary in shorts to enter a car that had been standing in the sun for any length of time. The seats and backrests would be unbearably hot to touch. One rapidly developed a special technique for handling such situations. By bracing the back against the seat with the feet on the floor, and pushing hard in both directions it was possible to keep the backs of the legs off the seat. Until the surface of the seat had cooled sufficiently to be bearable, it was necessary to drive the car in this 'wrestlers bridge' position. The toes were used to operate the pedals, while the heels exerted sufficient pressure on the floor to keep the back of the legs away from the hot surface of the seat.

Once the car was in motion, the searing desert air blowing through the open car window would burn the skin and dry the eyes until they burnt and stung. Consequently, during the heat of the summer, one drove the car with windows partially closed to divert the scorching air away from any exposed skin. Optimum comfort was a matter of balancing the bearable heat of the car interior against the searing draught from the windows.

When taking a trip into the desert, either on business or pleasure, it was common practice to inform the police, and possibly a friend as a backup measure. It was the height of foolishness to travel any distance from the town without giving some reliable person details of the time of departure, the route and destination, as well as an estimated time of return. This simple procedure saved many lives, particularly amongst the oil company workers who spent much of the time driving across open desert, far from hardtop roads and the more frequently used desert tracks.

Whenever driving in the desert it was advisable to carry at least one jerry can of 'sweet' water. This was intended not so much for drinking purposes as to replenish the car's cooling system should it require refilling. Without the use of the vehicle, one would be in serious trouble in the desert. A jerry can of water, a shovel and a piece of matting to place beneath the wheels, in case the car became bogged down in soft sand, were life saving essentials for the desert motorist.

In case of a breakdown, it was always advisable to stay with the car and remain quietly in the shade it provided. It was essential to conserve energy and prevent the loss of precious moisture by undue perspiration. To leave the vehicle and try to walk for assistance, even for short distances, was the height of folly. Any exertion encouraged dehydration and possible heat stroke. If help did not arrive immediately, the heat stroke victim would collapse and fall into a coma. The body temperature would rise uncontrollably leading to possible brain damage and finally death. In those early days, many fatalities occurred as a result of the occupants leaving their vehicles in a panic and attempting to walk for assistance.

During the period from mid-May to mid-July, a strong northerly wind, the Shamal, blew fitfully during the day between 10.00 a.m. and 4.00 p.m. It brought fine, airborne dust and intense heat to the desert. At such times, the poor visibility in the blowing dust resulted in many vehicles driving off the ill-defined desert tracks and becoming bogged down in soft sand. In a number of cases the occupants, rather then remaining with the car, sheltering from the heat and the dust until help arrived, would wander off in the hope of flagging down a passing car or finding some shelter from the heat. Inevitably, within a short period of exposure to the heat and the hot, dry, dust-laden wind, they would collapse from heat exhaustion. Unless they were found quickly, they would dehydrate and die a terrible death. Ironically, in many instances they were sometimes only a short distance from help.

The Shamal blew steadily throughout the months of May and June, carrying clouds of fine dust and sand over many hundreds of miles. The fine dust permeated everywhere, affecting visibility, irritating the eyes, infiltrating the food supplies and coating everything with a fine flour-like deposit.

The desert wind also picks up heavier sand particles. On particularly windy days, these flying particles would sandblast the paintwork of cars; removing the paint down to bare metal within minutes, scouring their windscreens and lamps until they were as opaque as frosted glass and necessitating their immediate replacement. Many people working in the desert had to replace the windscreens and headlamps of their cars as a matter of routine each year.

The desert tracks offered two types of surface, neither of them pleasant. One was a soft, treacherous, sandy surface over which a driver had to keep his vehicle moving at all costs. Should he stop or falter for an instant, the wheels would lose traction and the car would bed down into the soft sand.

The second type of surface was formed by gatch, the calcium sulphate rich, clay-like material, which was iron hard in the dry season. When the rains came, the material took on the consistency of a rich, creamy mud.

On commonly used tracks, this iron-hard material inexplicably formed itself into ripples similar to the sand ripples seen on a beach as the tide recedes, shaking the car and its occupants in an unbearable manner. Slow driving caused every single ripple to be felt with bone-jarring clarity. On the other hand, speeding over the ripples was considerably more comfortable for the passengers, but general wear and tear on the vehicle was accelerated to an unacceptable extent. Broken shock absorbers, suspensions and steering linkage failures were commonplace in those days.

At times the intense heat and flying dust made life out-of-doors almost unbearable. Consequently, after the novelty of continuous sunshine had abated, most expatriates, like the local Kuwaitis, stayed out of the sun whenever possible and fled during the heat of the day to the relatively cool surroundings of their homes for a regular afternoon siesta.

Around 4.30 p.m., when the sun's rays had lost their aggressive bite, people would begin to reappear. The locals would reopen their shops and the *souk* would burst into life again. It was then that many expatriates made their way down to the shops or to the beach for a late afternoon swim before returning home for dinner and the evening's social round.

The Kuwait beaches in those early years were delightful. Mile after mile of fine white sand, sloping gently to the clear, brilliant blue waters of Kuwait Bay, or further to the south, the Arabian Gulf. In spite of the extremely fast tidal flows bathing from most beaches was safe. There were the usual perils of tropical beaches in the form of sharks, barracuda, moray eels, stone fish, scorpion fish, lion fish and the dreaded Portuguese man-of-war, but there were few incidents and even fewer fatalities. As an added spice of danger, there were many sea snakes in the Gulf, but again there were no recorded fatalities resulting from bites by these extremely venomous creatures.

After experiencing the cold, murky waters around the British Isles, the clean, white beaches and the warm, crystal clear waters of the Gulf were a delight to the European expatriates. Consequently, the majority of the British community spent their free time at the beach or in the water.

In addition to the swimming and sunbathing, there were two yacht clubs and a power boat club, all with extremely active memberships. Thursday and Friday were racing days and there was always an excellent turn out. The wives and families stayed on the beach or prepared lunch, while the active sailors raced their dinghies around preset courses.

I was to find that it was so different in winter, when a cold north wind blew, cutting one like a whetted knife. During the day, the sun shone brilliantly from a cloudless sky providing a fitful warmth. After dusk, once the sun fell below the horizon, the cloudless desert sky rapidly absorbed what remained of the day's warmth. The air temperature would fall to freezing in the desert and the bedouin would huddle in their blankets around camp fires of camel dung. In the city, the locals would move around swathed in heavy coats and blankets, their faces muffled in woollen scarves.

In the winter period, beach picnics were popular on the more remote sections of the coast, which were too far away to be reached in the heat of the summer. Each Friday, after an early start, convoys of cars would leave Kuwait City, driving across the desert to the beaches at Shuiabah, Mina Saud, Salmiah or 'Slave's Castle'. The latter was a rocky headland where, it was said, slaves had been landed in the old days prior to being dispatched into the interior.

These idyllic days would be spent swimming, snorkelling and sunbathing. Homemade griddles, heated by burning charcoal, were used to barbecue steaks and chicken or reheat curries prepared the previous day. In the late afternoon the convoys would return with their tired, sunburnt and dehydrated cargoes of humanity. An ice cold beer from the refrigerator, a shower, a change of clothing and it was time for the cinema!

Unlike most of the Arabian peninsula, which

experiences a truly desert climate with extremely hot days and cool clear nights, Kuwait did not cool down as the sun set. The warm shallow water of Kuwait Bay and the Arabian Gulf, thirty-five degrees centigrade in summer, carried the heat of the day well into the night. Throughout the summer months, until early October, the moist heat from the warm waters of the shallow bay kept the town and coastal area in the clutches of a hot, damp humidity. It was only in the early hours of the morning, just before dawn, that a respite from the oppresive, moist heat could be noticed.

At the not infrequent times, when the air conditioning failed, the afternoon siesta and the early evenings were to be dreaded. At these times, one would stretch out on the bed in a pool of perspiration, or sit naked in a chair beneath the whirling ceiling fan which circulated the hot humid air round the room with little or no cooling effect. Without air conditioning, it was almost impossible to fall asleep before the early hours of the morning. Then after a few short minutes of fitful sleep, it was time to get up and go to work.

In those early days Kuwait had the luxury of two water supplies. A piped supply of high salinity brackish water used for washing and flushing toilets, and a supply of fresh water from the distillation plant for drinking purposes. The brackish water supply crossed the desert by pipeline from the Sulaibiyah well field, while the latter supply was delivered in rationed quantities by road tanker.

The potable water supply was loaded from large overhead storage tanks, located at strategic points around the city, into road tankers or bowsers. The bowsers distributed the water to the various houses. Each house had an overhead galvanized storage tank which was topped up on alternate days.

One could never be sure for what purpose the road tanker delivering the water had previously been used. Secondly, it was a common sight to see the bowser driver during his pre-prayer time ablutions washing his feet in the manhole on the top of the tanker. Consequently, it was wise to boil all drinking water; cooling it in the refrigerator before use.

As both the brackish and the potable water systems were exposed to the heat of the sun throughout the day, the water was extremely hot, almost unbearable to touch, by the time it reached the tap. In order to obtain water cool enough for a cold shower during the summer, it was common practice to turn off the power to the electric water heaters and use the water from the hot system as a cold supply, and the brackish water and the supply from the cold tap in place of the hot water system.

Empty gin bottles of which there appeared to be an endless supply, were usually used to store the drinking water in the refrigerator. There were many uncorroborated stories of servants accidentally returning full gin bottles to the refrigerator by mistake, resulting in some unfortunate teetotaller, devout Muslim or other innocent, drinking a tumbler full of ice cold gin without realizing it. Such stories abounded, always adding interest and contributing to the conversational topics around the dinner table in the mess or the club bar.

The intense heat of the Kuwaiti summer lasted from early May until mid-September. The bedouins claimed that the appearance of the Dog Star in the sky heralded the end of summer. This certainly appeared to be the case. When the Dog Star appeared in the evening sky, there was a noticeable reduction in the intensity of the midday heat, and nights became colder, presenting a pleasant relief.

As the weather became colder, usually around late October or early November, a series of violent thunderstorms together with intense tropical downpours would occur. These short, but intense storms would bring life in Kuwait to a complete standstill. The absence of an adequate drainage system aggravated the situation. The unmade roads in the city became waterlogged within minutes of the downpour starting. Cars became stuck in the cream-like mud formed by the wet gatch or, as in the case of Volkswagen Beetles, simply floated away on the flood waters.

The old Kuwaiti houses, made of sun baked mud or gatch that were so cool in the heat of the sun, leaked badly in even the slightest shower of rain. The electric wiring in many of these older buildings was totally inadequate. The insulation was non-existent and the wiring overloaded by the addition of air conditioning and other applicances, which were never envisioned when the original wiring was installed. At such times, these buildings became literally death traps, many tragic accidents occurred during the rains as a result of the faulty electrical connections.

Within a few days of the passing of the storm, the flood water dried up, but not before it triggered the growth of plants and grasses that had laid dormant throughout the desert summer. Within a matter of days the desert turned a bright fresh green. Myriads of brightly-coloured desert flowers bloomed for a short period of glory. For a few short days it was a delight to be out in the crisp cool air of the flowering desert. Unfortunately, good things pass, many too quickly. It was not long before the desert returned to its normal apparel of bare sandy gravel, spotted with sparse patches of camel thorn and scrub grass. The grasses and flowers were gone as though they had never been.

Their seeds were still there though just below the surface, waiting for the next rain to trigger their reappearance on the desert stage.

The cool season soon established itself. Although the days were still warm and sunny, the nights were cold and clear. Inland the cloudless starlit skies prompted heavy desert frosts, but in Kuwait near the coast, the north or northeasterly prevailing winds were chilly but not bitterly cold. At times though, the temperatures would drop below freezing. On the day following such a frost, it was a common sight to see line after line of cars stranded at the wayside with leaking radiators.

It was a delight to be in Kuwait during the cool period of the year. The sparkling weather remained until the end of March when once again a series of storms would herald a change in the weather, and the heat of the summer would begin to develop once again.

In spite of the difficult climatic conditions, life in those early days in Kuwait was tolerable at the worst, and at the best rewarding and enjoyable. My new life-style was full of interest and excitement. There was always something new to see or do. The beaches and the sea were wonderful to someone who had only previously experienced the pleasures of Blackpool and Southport, while the people I met during my work and leisure were an unending source of interest and fascination.

The majority of the early expatriates played a major role in the development of Kuwait, and contributed to its success to a degree not fully appreciated either by the expatriates who followed them, or by the Kuwaitis themselves.

With few exceptions the expatriate community was composed of pleasant, hard working, hospitable people. Many in their own right, were larger than life

47

characters, playing their role in life as they envisaged it to be. Others deliberately emphasized peculiarities to make themselves more noticeable in the social whirl. A few of the expatriate community were freewheelers and parasites, living off the efforts of the majority and taking more than they contributed in both effort and productivity.

I found all these people fascinating. My previous experiences in the UK as a nine to five worker in a nationalized industry had not prepared me to meet the assortment of eccentrics, individualists and unusual personalities that abounded in Kuwait at that time.

3

A Short History Of Kuwait

As time went by, I had the opportunity to learn more of my employers and their small desert country which was approximately the size of Wales in the UK.

Kuwait is a wedge shaped section of the Arabian peninsula, located along the north-western shore of the Arabian or Persian Gulf. The Sheikhdom extends approximately 120 miles from north to south and 100 miles from east to west, covering an area of some 6,000 square miles. It is bounded to the north and northwest by Iraq, to the south and southwest by Saudi Arabia and to the east by the Persian or Arabian Gulf.

The City of Kuwait is located on the southeastern shore of Kuwait Bay, a large sheltered area of water which forms a natural harbour for the state.

In the eighteenth century, approximately 1710 AD, a severe and prolonged drought drove the Bani Utub tribe of bedouins, led by the Al-Sabah and Al-Khalifah families, southward from the inner Nadj in the north of the Arabian peninsula to Al-Duwasir int he south. Conditions were found to be no better there and the tribes moved on to Zubara in the Qatar peninsula, only to find that the drought was well established in that area also.

Finally, the tribes moved northwards again. This time along the coastal plain, until they arrived at a headland fronting a large bay. Here, by digging shallow surface wells, they found sufficient sweet water for their flocks. Tired of wandering, they settled in this area, the site of the present City of Kuwait. Gradually, the bedouins of the Bani Utub tribe forsook their tents and built houses, gradually establishing a town on the site of the modern City of Kuwait.

Some years later, a threatened invasion by the Al-Nasar tribe from Arabistan resulted in the Al-Khalifah family and their followers leaving the settlement. They moved southwards away from the threatened area of conflict. Initially, they returned to Qatar, but later for security they moved on to Bahrain Island, where they settled and prospered. Finally they became accepted as the ruling family on the Island, which they remain to this day.

The threatened invasion of Kuwait was quelled by Salim Ibn Muhammed Al-Sabah, a strong ruthless leader, who led an armed expeditionary force to the camp of the Al-Nasars. They carried out a surprise attack, defeating the Al-Nasar fleet of armed dhows. After this decisive battle, Kuwait became established as the permanent home of the Al-Sabah tribe and their dependent families.

Gradually, the previous inhabitants of the area, comprising small isolated groups of fishermen, accepted the rule of the Al-Sabah family, thus welding the small settlement into a united community. Many of the bedouins turned to fishing and pearling as their livelihood. A small dhow building industry was started and Kuwaiti crews sailed throughout the Gulf trading pearls and general goods. Rapidly, the small settlement began to gain prosperity and status in the area.

By 1764, according to the Danish explorer, Carsten Niebuhr, there were more than eight hundred boats based in Kuwait. They fished and traded throughout the Gulf and as far afield as the Indian and the African coasts. Gradually, Kuwait became famous as a pearling port and many Kuwaiti families made fortunes in the pearl industry, establishing international companies with offices as far afield as Bombay and Paris.

It is said that at this time the area was governed by the Sheikh of Al-Hasa, the Arabian coastal province which lies some distance to the south. The Al-Sabah family aspired to an independent state of their own. They were gradually able to attain this by negotiation and discussion with the powerful sheikhs and governors in the surrounding territories. Subsequently, one of the Sabah elders met with the Turkish Governor of Basrah and received his approval for the tribe to take up permanent residence on the land surrounding Kuwait Bay. Thus permanently establishing the independence and autonomy of the Sheikhdom of Kuwait.

In 1899 a treaty was signed between Britain and Sheikh Mubarak of the ruling Al-Sabah family in which Britain provided Kuwait with military protection in exchange for certain trading privileges. At the time, Britain was particularly interested in disrupting German and Turkish plans to drive a railroad from Constantinople through Mesopotamia, then Turkish Arabia, to the Gulf Coast.

A subsequent extension to this agreement confirmed that Kuwait would only allow British post offices controlled from the Indian office to operate within the Sheikhdom and would not grant pearl or sponge fishing concessions except by British consent. In 1913 a further clause not to grant oil concessions without British consent was also included in the general agreement.

In 1913, as a result of the Anglo-Turkish Agreement, which recognized Britain's special position in the Gulf and validity of Britain's treaties with Bahrain and Kuwait, the status and borders of Kuwait were confirmed and the autonomy of the Sheikh of Kuwait, as tribal overlord and ruler of the designated area of Kuwait, was officially recognized.

The history of modern Kuwait commenced with the rule of the Great Mubarak in 1896. Mubarak's brother, Muhammed, the Ruler, was a weak man and strongly influenced by Yusuf bin Abdullah Al-Ibrahim, a representative of the Turkish Governor of Basrah. When Mubarak objected to the Turkish influence in the Kuwaiti court, he was banished to the desert on the pretext of restoring order amongst the bedouins. Under cover of darkness he returned to Kuwait and assassinated both Sheikh Muhammed and his second brother, Jarrah. It is said that Mubarak could not kill his brother while he slept; he therefore awakened him before stabbing him to death, thus assuaging his honour. When the elders of Kuwait entered the Majilis room at the palace on the following morning they found Mubarak enthroned as their Sheikh.

Two attempts by the Turkish rulers of the Basrah province to depose Sheikh Mubarak failed miserably, confirming his position as Ruler and establishing him as a power to be reckoned with in the area. As a result of his friendship for Abdul Rahman Ibn Saud and his sympathy towards the Saud cause, Mubarak offered sanctuary from the Al-Rashid family, Rulers of the Najd, to Abdul Rahman and his young son, Abdul Aziz Ibn Saud. Some years later, Mubarak gave moral and physical support to the nineteen-year-old Abdul Aziz's successful expedition into Arabia where, on 14th

January 1902 he captured Riyadh.

In view of the recent Iraqi claims to Kuwait, it is important to note that Iraq did not become a self-governing entity until after the end of the First World War. Prior to this, it was a part of the Ottoman Empire and Kuwait's boundaries and sovereignity were already well established long before this! Consequently, Iraq has no basis for its claim of sovereignty over Kuwait.

There is no doubt, however, that after the formation of Iraq after the First World War, and the appointment of King Faisel as its Ruler in 1920, and the country's actual independence in 1932, Iraq cast avaricious eyes upon the natural harbour facilities available in Kuwait Bay, and the strategic position of Kuwait's Bubiyan Island situated at the mouth of the Shatt Al Arab River. No matter how logical Iraq's reasons for desiring Bubiyan Island and the deep water port on the Gulf, it does not constitute a right to annex a small independent country with absolutely no aggressive intent towards its neighbours.

In 1925, the Eastern and General Syndicate, a British company established by Major Frank Holmes, obtained concessions to drill for oil in Bahrain. Subsequently, on 23rd December 1934, the Sheikh of Kuwait, H.H. Ahmad Al-Jabir, granted a seventy-five-year concession to the Kuwait Oil Company, a joint venture company formed between the Anglo-Iranian Oil Company and the Eastern Gulf Oil Company of the USA.

Drilling for oil commenced in 1936. The second well drilled at Burgan struck oil and development of the field commenced. At the outbreak of war in 1939, development of the field was suspended and existing wells were sealed off. It was not until 1946 that the field was reopened and the first cargo of Kuwait oil was loaded onto a tanker for overseas delivery.

The reopening of the Kuwait oilfields signalled a phase of unparalleled development. A 4,100 foot long pier with eight tanker loading berths and a further six submarine loading lines was constructed in record time at Mina Al-Ahmadi, the oil port located some twenty-six miles south of Kuwait City. A 30,000 barrel per day refinery, including a steam power station and a seawater desalination plant were built in an area adjacent to the pier. Further inland, some five hundred feet above the coast, a small residential township, named Ahmadi to commemorate the name of the late Sheikh, was constructed to house the thousand expatriate employees of the company. With this infrastructure in place, the development of the oilfields proceeded at an unprecedented pace.

In 1948 oil development was commenced in the Neutral Zone, a buffer area along Kuwait's southern borders with Saudi Arabia, jointly administered by the two countries. The American Independent Oil Company and the Western Pacific Company (the latter owned by Paul Getty) commenced drilling operations. Subsequently, a further concession was given to the Arabian Oil Company, a Japanese company. Revenue from these sources was shared between Kuwait and Saudi Arabia.

In the 1930s the population of Kuwait was less than 60,000. Upon development of the oil resources in the late 1940s the population rose to approximately 100,000 people. When I arrived in 1954 the population of the small state had already grown to 200,000. This growth continued throughout the years until prior to the Iraqi invasion of 1990 it totalled over 2,000,000, with true Kuwait nationals numbering less than 500,000. Over the years, many foreign nationals owed their livelihood and prosperity to the magnanimity of the Kuwaitis who provided work, shelter and more than fair wages for their services.

Kuwait's fresh water wells had long since been depleted and were unable to meet the demands of the growing city for drinking water. A group of entrepreneurial captains met the demand for drinking water by importing fresh water from the Shatt Al-Arab River.

Their dhows would cast anchor in the delta north of Bubiyan Island and they filled their tanks with the relatively fresh river water. Once the tanks were full, they would sail back to Kuwait and sit at anchor for a day or so in Kuwait Bay, allowing the silt and dirt to settle from the water. They would then pump the semi-clear water into the Sheikh's tank, a circular steel tank erected close to the shore at Shuwaikh. Shortly after my arrival this tank collapsed as a result of the severe corrosion that had developed over the years in service with the corrosive river water.

Earlier, as a gesture of good will, the Kuwait Oil Company converted a disused oil line to carry a small quantity of distilled water from the Ahmadi storage tanks to the Sheikh's tank at Shuwaikh. So impressed was Sheikh Abdullah Al-Salim, the Ruler, with the quality and purity of the desalinated water, that he instructed that a one million gallons per day capacity desalination plant and steam power station be erected near the city, in the Shuwaikh area, to provide drinking water and electricity for the people of Kuwait.

This plant was completed in 1953. The adequate supplies of fresh water and electricty heralded an immediate improvement in the standard of living and quality of life of the Kuwait people. As the population and standards of living increased, additional plant was installed, the Government always ensuring that the Kuwaiti people had adequate supplies of power and pure water available for their needs.

Unlike the average bedouin, the Kuwaiti people, like the Omanis, had been sailors and traders for over two centuries. Their exposure to many different cultures from Africa to India, as well as British, Dutch and Portuguese traders, gave them an appreciation and tolerance not generally present in the more austere philosophy of the bedouin tribes of the Arabian peninsula.

One cannot but be amazed at the ease with which the simple unsophisticated Kuwaitis adapted to the sudden growth of oil wealth and the subsequent increasing complexity of life in the city. Over a few short years, simple merchants of the *souk,* after a lifetime of buying and selling goods valued at a few rupees, evolved into sophisticated financiers dealing in millions of dollars. Yet throughout this transition, the majority of Kuwaitis remained a simple, unpretentious people, kind and considerate, loyal to their old friends and always willing to help worthwhile causes. There were exceptions to this of course, but this does not detract from the truth of the above observation.

4

Ali Al-Kettle

One of the first people I met when I first arrived in Kuwait was a charge engineer named Ted. He worked in the operations section of the desalination plant at Shuwaikh. He was a pleasant looking man of medium height with a well clipped naval beard, a legacy of his past as a sea-going engineer.

A devoted family man with a wife, two children and a mother-in-law, his whole life revolved around their wellbeing. They lived in a Swedish style, prefabricated bungalow at Sulaibikhat, the Government residential camp for married families. Ted rarely drank and was particularly abstemious at parties attended by senior officials or management. Being inclined to be something of a social climber and extremely position conscious, he would do nothing which might cause criticism by higher authority.

He also had a considerable reputation as a magpie, a compulsive collector of junk! Reputedly, he would confiscate anything left lying around that he might think would be useful to him at some time. The greater part of his time at work was spent strolling around the plant keeping a weather eye open for any odd pieces of wire, screws or anything that might be useful to him in the future, and was not actually tied down.

Ted was an enthusiastic and talented sailor. Although he was a member of the local yacht club and sailed regularly at weekends, he was particularly fond of power boats and had built his own motor boat from a kit. The boat, a sixteen foot fibre glass ski-boat with a powerful outboard motor, was called *Lady Enid* after his wife.

The *Lady Enid* was his pride and joy and he spent many loving hours each week preparing the boat for the weekend. It was his great delight to sail down to the Sheikh's beach close to the Dasman Palace and provide water ski rides for his own family and any of the bathers who were prepared to risk life and limb being towed at high speed behind the *Lady Enid.*

By chance, Ted acquired a second boat, a locally built launch made from heavy gauge steel. The steel boat was extremely heavy and had little buoyancy; it was in fact quite dangerous, with little free board. Consequently, it could easily be swamped in moderately heavy seas. It required a powerful outboard to drive it through the water, which further added to its buoyancy problems. Knowing that it would be impossible to sell the boat to the more experienced sailors, he attempted to sell this boat to inexperienced new arrivals; greedily demanding an exorbitant price. Fortunately, because of the high price Ted was asking, he was never able to find a purchaser!

Ted was extremely proud of his sea-going associations and made a point of cultivating the persona that he believed to be typical of a master mariner. He grew a naval type beard and cultivated a loud, aggressive and commanding telephone voice! When he spoke, it was almost to the point of rudeness, we unkindly described it as his 'Captain on the Bridge' voice! It was jokingly claimed that Ted did not really require a telephone at all, the other party could hear him without the aid of the instrument.

As might be expected, Ted was particularly sensitive regarding his appearance and the maintenance of his nautical ambience. So much so, that he was reluctant to wear spectacles even though his eyesight was quite poor. This reluctance on his part to wear glasses might easily have been responsible for the wrong button being pressed during an emergency situation at the plant, causing an interruption to the power supply to the city. At least, that is what Dick Jones, his senior charge engineer, claimed! Dick never let Ted forget the incident.

Dick Jones, a chubby, aggressive Welshman, the senior charge engineer on Ted's shift, was a difficult man to work with at the best of times. A qualified power station engineer who had worked his way up via night school, he objected strongly to Ted's superior, 'Naval Commander' attitude. Consequently, he stated openly that he hated all things naval with an illogical intensity. To have assigned Ted to the same shift as Dick was either a serious error of management or a masterful stroke of cruel vengeance.

After a few weeks on shift with Dick, Ted was reduced to a quaking shadow of his former self. Dick pulled rank outrageously. Overawed by Dick's strength of character and superior technical ability, Ted was putty in his hands.

During the night shift when there was little to do other than make a periodic tour of inspection, Dick took great delight in setting Ted impromptu examinations. He would gravely place a pad and pencil in front of Ted and commence asking detailed technical questions relating to the plant layout, operational procedures and general electrical and mechanical theory. He demanded that Ted draw pipe layouts, electrical circuits and plant locations to illustrate his answers.

During the day shift, when it was not possible to spend time on written tests, Dick would invent other methods to plague Ted. Whenever he saw Ted without his glasses, his favourite ploy was to subject Ted to an impromptu eye test!

As they walked around the plant, Dick would stop and demand that Ted cover one eye and read out loud the words on a notice, the script on a panel label or a valve name plate. He would then, with great ceremony, laboriously write down Ted's interpretation prior to walking over to the test piece in order to compare Ted's statement with the actual wording.

Dick would then issue Ted with a signed, 'Official Test Certificate', pointing out any mistakes that Ted may have made. When Ted was correct in his answer, the crestfallen look on Dick's face was reward enough for Ted to continue to submit to these demoralizing tests. He took as much delight in Dick's chagrin when he was able to provide a correct answer as Dick did when Ted failed. It didn't take long for the sympathy for Ted to fade and for the opinion of the rest of the staff to crystalize in the assumption that they deserved each other!

Shortly after my arrival in Kuwait, I developed a routine which included a morning visit to the charge engineer's office to read the Operations Log Book report for the previous night, and to enjoy a cup of tea and chat with the particular engineers on shift at the time.

One morning I arrived at the charge engineer's office to be met by the long faces of the shift engineer and his assistant. They had been on shift for four hours and had not been able to have a cup of tea! The kettle, normally a permanent fixture in the office, was missing. The previous night shift had reported the loss after being forced to face a tealess night. They had looked in vain and despite a detailed search of the whole plant, the kettle had not been recovered. It was their opinion that it had been deliberately removed.

Immediately, an investigation was started to locate the kettle and rectify this serious state of affairs. It did not take long to discover that the shift engineer's kettle had been purloined by Ted! He had appropriated the kettle from the shift office during the afternoon shift. One of the maintenance foremen had seen him placing it in his car.

When asked, Ted denied any knowledge of the kettle, but of course no-one believed him. We all knew him for the magpie he was and suspected the worst.

The following day, I invited the engineers to the laboratory where Haji plied them with cups of hot sweet tea until their morale returned. We then set about the problem of determining how best to regain custody of the kettle. Ted's character was discussed at great length in a most uncomplimentary manner by his colleagues, and a plot was hatched to teach him a lesson.

Some two months previously, during the commissioning of the plant, the consulting engineers had installed an electric wall clock in the control room of the plant. The clock had disappeared after the commissioning period. No-one knew for certain, but all assumed that somehow the clock had found its way into Ted's possession, to be joined later by the kettle.

Our plan was simple! We drafted a letter on official stationery addressed to Ted and allegedly from the

Ministry of Public Works' Department of Housing and Property. It stated that it had come to the notice of the Housing Department, through an informant, that Ted had unlawfully taken possession of a wall clock and a kettle which had been issued by the Department to the power and desalination plant. These items were included in the Department's inventory and were an official part of the power and desalination plant equipment. The letter continued that providing the two items were returned by the end of the month, no further action would be taken. The letter was closed and signed in Arabic, using the Arabic *nom de plume,* 'Ali El Kettle El Clock'! We placed the letter in an official envelope addressed to Ted and left it in the mail distribution box.

The following day, when the mail was distributed, we all made a point of being in the office when Ted arrived. Instead of leaving after collecting our mail from the distribution box, we all stood around chatting together, but covertly watching Ted. We were disappointed! Ted read the letter without comment and left.

This was an anticlimax. We had at least hoped for a show of anger or dismay. It was felt that Ted had not taken the bait, and the incident was forgotten.

How wrong we were! Some three weeks later Ted slipped into my office carrying two large packages. He asked to speak to me in confidence with regard to a problem that he had. Over a cup of tea and a biscuit, he confessed all. Apparently after receiving the letter, he had tried to return the clock and the kettle to the Ministry of Public Works. Something we had not expected.

He had been referred from office to office and department to department, but no-one would accept the clock or the kettle. After three weeks of this he was becoming quite desperate. No-one would accept either of the items from Ted. None of the clerks concerned would admit not having any knowledge of the case, they all gave Ted the impression that they knew of the letter, but could not accept the clock or the kettle as it was not in their department. Ted was sure that the letter was genuine and had become more and more disturbed as time passed.

He was convinced that unless he could return the items to someone in authority, an official complaint would be received by the Chief Engineer, leading to possible dismissal or even a court case. I felt quite sorry for him, but he was so emotionally charged that I could not tell him the whole thing was a joke.

After some thought, I suggested that in my opinion, he should return the items to their proper places in the control room and the shift engineer's office, and then write to the Ministry to inform them that the items had been restored to their proper places. Then the Ministry would in all probability be quite satisfied and probably nothing further would be heard.

Ted jumped at the suggestion. That same afternoon the clock was back on the wall in the control room, and the kettle was once again boiling away on the tea table in the shift office. Within a week Ted was his old self again. He never did get a reply to his letter! No doubt the clerks in the Ministry stores shook their heads in wonder, marvelling at the crazy Englishman taking the trouble to inform them that a clock was on the wall in the control room and a kettle was in the shift engineer's office again. Fortunately, no-one followed it up, and Ted never discovered the practical joke we had played upon him.

5

The Lost Weekend

Each year in May, as the summer heat commenced to replace the pleasant warmth of the Kuwait spring, expatriate females and their young families commenced their annual migration back to more temperate climes! Usually, the mass exodus coincided with the conclusion of the school year and by early June only a few hardy ladies remained.

It was a difficult time for the men. They were used to having their families with them. Unlike the single men in the bachelor camps at Shuwaikh and Sulaibikhat, they were not self-sufficient and the departure of their families left them lonely and confused. They haunted the bars, drank too much and ate too little. In over-compensation for their loneliness, they threw parties, organized beach barbecues and usually made a thorough nuisance of themselves until it was time for their summer leave, when they departed to join their families once again.

The desalination plant staff were no exception. Fred McKenzie the Deputy Plant Superintendent, Jock Sutherland the Electrical Engineer, John Peacock the Operations Engineer, Bob Thwaites and Ted both shift engineers, were all bachelors as a result of the summer exodus. Like the others, when their families left, they were at a loss to fill the empty hours between work and sleep.

As a group, they took it in turns to entertain their friends and colleagues to dinner before retiring to the cinema, tombola, the weekend dance or the club bar. On Thursdays and Fridays the menu was always curry, but during the week the imagination was given free rein. Each in his turn attempted to outdo the efforts of the previous host. As a friend of the group, I was always invited. Many pleasant meals were shared with them, and one was never bored with the conversation.

One particular Friday, John Peacock decided that it was his turn to entertain us. When I arrived at 12.00 noon the party was well under way. The drinks had been flowing freely, and with the exception of John, who was busy in the kitchen, all were well lubricated. After an excellent lunch we sat down for coffee and conversation before returning home for the usual afternoon siesta. Fred, Jock, Bob and Ted decided against coffee and settled down to some serious drinking.

Sometime later, Jock and Fred were heatedly debating the finer points of the battles of Bonnie Prince Charlie with the English Redcoats, while Bob Thwaites had joined John and myself at the coffee table. Ted was silent, gazing deeply into space; probably on the bridge of an imaginary destroyer, guiding his trusty ship through an enemy minefield (or could he possibly be wondering if the clock and kettle incident would unexpectedly raise its head again?).

Suddenly, with the intention of showing Fred how the Highlanders fought at the battle of Culloden Moor, Jock leapt to his feet with a wild shout waving an imaginary claymore above his head. The effort was too much! He tottered, tried to regain his balance, and fell forward, face down, across the settee!

Fred, taking note of Jock's plight, and deciding that he also had had enough to drink, rose to his feet and said that he was going home. With this prompt, Bob and I also rose to leave. Ted sat oblivious to it all, still gazing into space.

It was obvious that the more serious casualties could not drive. John said that he would take Ted home, and Bob and I offered to take Jock and Fred back to Shuwaikh. Fred, who had an unbelievable capacity for drink, said that he was fine, and would deliver Jock back home. Prior to leaving and going our separate ways, Jock insisted that we meet at his house that evening for a sandwich, before going on to the cinema.

Finally, after some little difficulty, everyone was marshalled into their various vehicles. John had difficulty getting Ted into his car, but finally succeeded and drove him away. Bob Thwaites and I followed Fred McKenzie's rather erratic course to Jock's bungalow, after one or two close shaves with a roundabout and the curb at corners in the road. Upon arriving home, Fred wisely decided not to put his car in the garage, waved to us and went inside.

That evening, as scheduled, we met in Jock's house. Bob, Fred, John and myself arrived in good time, but Ted never appeared. We telephoned his house, but there was no answer.

Jock had made some ham sandwiches and opened a can of fruit for dessert. We were all hungry and the food was quickly finished. John offered to help by opening another tin of ham and making a few more sandwiches. He brought in the plate of sandwiches and casually asked Jock where he should put the empty tin and the wrapping papers. Jock was surprised to learn that the ham slices were individually wrapped! Apparently, our first helping of sandwiches had an additional bonus of paper as well as the ham. None of us had noticed!

The following day at work, we learned of Ted's afternoon adventures. Sometime after John had dropped him off at his bungalow, Mohammed, the Chief Clerk at the desalination plant, passed by. Hearing a strange noise from the garden, he looked over the tamarisk hedge. He was horrified and concerned to see Ted lying naked in the middle of the lawn.

Mohammed in his innocence, assumed that Ted had been suddenly taken ill and rushed into the garden to help. He washed Ted down with the garden hose then dried him off with towels from the bathroom. When Ted was clean and dry, Mohammed dragged him into the house and managed to get him onto the bed. This was no mean feat, Ted was a big man and Mohammed quite frail by comparison.

As Mohammed was about to cover Ted with a bed sheet, because the air conditioned house was quite cool, Ted regained consciousness. Making a remarkable recovery and with no prior warning, he leapt out of bed with a roar. He accused Mohammed of trying to interfere with him. Then, aiming a wild blow at Mohammed, he leapt at him. Mohammed fled for his life!

Ted chased him around the house, roaring and shouting all the while. Finally Mohammed managed to dart into the bathroom and lock himself in. Ted hammered on the door until Mohammed was convinced that the lock would break.

After some considerable time the hammering on the door ceased and the house became quiet. Mohammed, too terrified to leave, remained in the bathroom for almost three hours. Finally, hearing the telephone ringing unanswered, he assumed that Ted had left the house. This gave him the courage to open the bathroom door and escape. As he tiptoed past the bedroom he heard Ted snoring. Glancing through the open bedroom door, he saw Ted stretched out on the bed, sleeping as soundly as a baby. Mohammed crept out of the house and fled away as fast as he could.

Naturally, this was the major topic of conversation at the plant for the next few days. Mohammed complained to Pop Demain, the plant Superintendent, that Ted had attacked and tried to murder him. He threatened to complain to the police unless Pop took some action. Ted, on the other hand, denied any knowledge of the incident.

After some time and many apologies had been lavished on Mohammed, the incident was forgotten officially. Ted had learnt his lesson however, he never joined the group again for their regular drinks and lunch parties!

6

On The Beach

The Kuwait beaches were the centre of the expatriates' social activities. Every afternoon, between the hours of 4.00 and 5.30 p.m., when the heat of the day had passed, employees and their families would gather on the beach at Shuwaikh. On Friday, the local day of rest, the whole day was spent swimming, sunbathing and eating.

A regular visitor to a particular section of beach or picnic area rapidly became territorial. Within a short period of time, a sense of ownership developed. With few exceptions the same group of people used the same stretch of beach day after day and would guard their section of beach as jealously as an old bull seal at mating time!

Should strangers be so unwise as to stray onto a section of occupied beach without invitation, they were immediately regarded with open hostility by the regular beach resident. The beach regular would immediately rouse himself, sit up and pointedly watch the new arrivals until they departed, overcome by the negative vibrations emanating in their direction.

Should the interlopers happen to be non-European expatriates, the suspicious stare would turn to open hostility! Foreign Arabs were regarded with the deepest of suspicion. Rightly or wrongly, it was assuaged that they had no interest in the sea or the beach, but only came to watch the crazy Westerners broiling themselves in the heat of the sun, or to cast a furtive glance at the immodestly clad (by Islamic standards) western ladies on the family beaches.

Needless to say, one rarely saw a Kuwaiti on the beach. Like most sailors, they loved boats and sailing, but had great reluctance to actually enter the water and were not particularly fond of swimming. The Kuwaitis had a great seafaring tradition, building and sailing their own fleet of seagoing dhows. In their heyday as mariners, they sailed as far afield as India and the West Coast of Africa. They, like their brethren further down the Gulf in the Emirates and Oman, were gold smugglers, pearl and spice traders.

After a few days spent investigating the beach, I located a place for myself on an old swimming raft that had been stranded some ten metres from the high tide line. The old raft was ideal for sunbathing. It was free from sand, and I could leave my clothes on it without them getting full of grit and dust. The air space between the deck and the relatively cool sand in the shade beneath the timbers allowed a cool draught to blow upwards between the boards, a most valuable asset in the heat of summer.

Surprisingly, until my arrival, no-one had claimed this old raft as their territory. I was therefore able to take up residence without upsetting anyone. Within a short time, the raft location became associated with me. Should anyone wish to reach me during 'Beach Hours', it was assumed that I could be found at the old raft on Shuwaikh Beach.

My closest neighbours along the beach were a group

of Italian and Greek expatriates, who for all intents and purposes, appeared to live on the beach. They were always there when I arrived and were still there, swimming and sunbathing, when I left. The group included four Italians and five Greeks, but their numbers would often swell with similar nationalities during beach parties and barbecues.

The Vatistas family formed the Greek section of the group. They were gregarious and fun loving, playing hard and working even harder. The men all worked for private companies in the town.

Charlie, the elder brother, was manager of the Abdullah Mullah Travel Agency. He worked 24-hours a day, seven days a week, drumming up business for the travel agency and the KLM Airline whom they represented. Charlie would move from expatriate to expatriate, passing the time of day and alerting them to any special offers of cheap flights or excursions. He would find out when anyone was due to take their annual leave, then would make a point of offering them cheap tickets and special tours that might be of interest to them. Needless to say, he was highly thought of by the Al-Mullah organization which he served so admirably.

Vango Vatistas, the younger brother, played football for the Shuwaikh Camp team and was an honorary member of the Camp Club. Consequently, the Vatistas were able to attend the various camp functions, including the weekend dances. They were generous to a fault. Whenever they attended a dance it was always as a family, champagne flowed like water at their table and there was a continuous exchange of drinks with other groups.

The Italian family, the second part of the group, was somewhat less gregarious and more reserved than their friends. They were nice people and well liked. Their daughter, Gabby, a single girl around twenty years of age, was extremely popular. Although rather plain of face, she had a superb figure. All the single males, both bachelors and married men in single status, gathered around her like bees around a honey pot. But to no avail! Gabby's parents kept them all at bay. Without being aggressive, they made it impossible for the many suitors to make any headway with her.

A regular member of the Italian group was Charles Spetzia, a short thickset gentleman with the profile and weathered features of an old and not too successful prizefighter. His nose had been broken a number of times, his ears, lips and facial skin was thickened and marked with numerous scars. His physique was robust to say the least. He must have weighed around 120 kg at five foot six inches in height. His huge neck, thick arms and barrel chest marked him as a man of great strength. He looked for all the world like a professional heavyweight wrestler.

Charles was employed at the Shuwaikh port. He was responsible for the maintenance of navigation and dredging equipment used to keep access to the port open for shipping and to mark the deep water channel.

On the beach, Charles always wore the same uniform. It comprised brilliantly coloured, long-legged swimming shorts which always appeared to be on the point of falling down, beach shoes, a large Panama hat, and a rainbow coloured Hawaiian beach shirt open to the waist. Wherever he was, at home in Shuwaikh Camp, on the beach or at work, Charles always wore his shirts completely unbuttoned and flapping around his ample waist. He would sit under a large sun umbrella which he always brought with him, or stand in the shallows gazing out to sea, sometimes he would walk up and down the water's edge. Although he spent so much time on the beach, he never swam.

Rumour had it that Charlie Spetzia had been involved in bootlegging in the days of prohibition. It was said that he had been deported from the USA for various antisocial activities. When he spoke English his accent was typical of Chicago and strongly reminiscent of the Edward G. Robinson type gangster films.

Charles always denied any knowledge of such activities, but while in his cups he would tell many anecdotes of the 'Old Days in Chicago', including tales of running battles with the police, bootlegging escapades and other colourful activities. In spite of this somewhat colourful past, Charles had a heart of gold and would help anyone whenever he was able. It was his willingness to be of service to anyone in need that was to influence his life and that of his family.

Paul Getty, the oil tycoon, had a small oilfield operation in the neutral zone between Kuwait and Saudi Arabia. The oil company, named The Western Pacific Oil Company, later to be called the Getty Oil Company, operated a well field at Wafra, some thirty-six miles from the coast and shipping terminal at Mina Saoud on the coast. It was during one of Paul Getty's visits to his oil installation that he met Charles.

Paul Getty had an inherent dislike of flying and he would only travel by ship or road. Whenever he came to Kuwait he would sail to Beirut and then drive along the trans-Arabian pipeline (TAP Line) road running from the Lebanon to Dharan in Saudi Arabia.

One day, by chance, Charles was driving along the desert track leading from Kuwait to the neutral zone when he came across a car deeply bogged down in the soft sand. Charles stopped and went back to offer assistance. The car was too deeply embedded to be pulled out without the help of a heavy truck. Kind hearted as usual, Charles offered to take the passengers on to Mina Saoud, their destination, even though it was considerably out of his way.

Charles had no idea who Paul Getty was. The oil company was known as Pacific Western at that time, and as far as he was concerned, Paul Getty was just another employee of the company. Charles, always gregarious, had no inhibitions in speaking about his own affairs. Consequently, by the time they reached Mina Saoud, Paul Getty knew all about Charles, his family in Italy and the difficulty Charles was having in finding work for his son.

After delivering Paul Getty and his companions to Mina Saoud, Charles thought no more about the incident. Some weeks later, he received a letter from his son to say that he had been approached with the offer of a job in the stores department of the Getty Oil Company in Italy!

Paul Getty maintained a personal interest in Charles's son, and as that worthy's knowledge of the oil industry developed, he was systematically promoted to positions of greater responsibility. Finally, he became manager of the Getty Oil Refinery in Italy. Some two years later, Charles left Kuwait and his job in the Shuwaikh port to join his son in the Getty organization.

Further along the beach, other families and groups had located themselves. One of these was the Cullen family. Matt and Bea Cullen together with their two daughters, Margie and Astrid, were regular visitors to the beach. Kindly, hospitable people, they were stalwarts of the local Scottish community.

74

Both Matt and Bea were members of various societies. Matt was for some time the President of the Caledonian Society. He delighted in presiding at the Burns Suppers, the various readings of Burns's poetry held throughout the year. He would give the address and loyal toast with great relish, reciting the poems in a great voice, heavy with dialect for the occasion.

Matt and Bea were active in the local drama society. Matt took part in the productions, while Bea assisted back stage as wardrobe mistress and make-up artist. Matt also played the drums in the John Shipton Band at the weekly Camp Club dances, while Bea sat patiently with friends throughout the evening.

The talent available in such a small community was quite extraordinary. Amongst the expatriates' wives were ex-dancers, professional singers – even a professional ice skater! With such talent on call, it was possible to produce many excellent plays and musicals.

As the one and only chemist, I found myself called upon to provide make-up and special effects for the various shows performed by the group. On request, I produced stage make-up, explosions, coloured flares, smoke etc. whenever called upon to do so! From time to time, various special effects were required, particularly for the annual pantomime for the children. Arranging these effects stretched one's ingenuity to the limit.

One particular production required a series of red and white flashes with clouds of coloured smoke. The good fairy would appear with a white flash while the Demon King would appear with a red flash. He would leap through the cloud of chemical smoke to wreak vengeance upon Mother Goose, to the delight of both the children and the adults! Matt, of course, was the ideal choice for the Demon King. He was quite magnificent in his scarlet tights, horned skull cap and golden trident.

Even though I say so myself, the effects for this show were most effective. A homemade formulation produced a brilliant red flash with clouds of crimson smoke for the Demon King, while a simple magnesium mixture provided a brilliant white flash for the Fairy Queen. The powder was placed in a series of silica crucibles set out on a board. The crucibles were fired at will by an electrical current passing through a piece of fuse wire set in the charge of flash powder in the crucible. A remote switch, corresponding to a particular crucible and operated by one of the volunteer stage hands, fired the charge.

Initially, all went well. However, as the week progressed the stage staff became more adventurous and daring. My prescribed quantity of the explosive charge was doubled, then trebled. The more the audience applauded the magnitude of the flash and the cloud of smoke as Matt appeared, the more the stage hands tried to improve upon success by providing more brilliant flashes and larger clouds of crimson smoke. On the final night of the show the stage staff excelled themselves! They must have completely filled the crucibles with the remainder of the flash powder.

As Matt made his first appearance there was a tremendous flash and a cloud of smoke. The Demon King appeared from the dense cloud of crimson smoke, his face blackened, his tights smouldering and glowing in numerous places. Frantically beating at smouldering areas on his tights, Matt fled from the stage.

The stage staff must have been supremely gratified. Matt's entry was the show stopper of the week. The audience were hysterical with laughter at his plight. Each time Matt appeared during the remainder of the show, the audience cheered and clapped, hoping for a repeat performance. Fortunately for his wellbeing, the stage staff had learnt their lesson and reverted to the correct charges for the flash pots.

Matt, like John Shipton, had been in the Middle East for a considerable time. Prior to taking a job with the Kuwait Ports Authority as Assistant Harbour Master, he had worked in both Iran and Iraq from the early thirties. He had been responsible for the maintenance of the navigational markers in the Shatt Al-Arab River. In Kuwait, Matt was in charge of the operation and maintenance of navigational aids, lights, markers and general maintenance of the port marine equipment.

Matt, as did most of the 'Old Timers', had a fund of anecdotes and stories; mostly related to the characters who worked in the Gulf, servicing the lights and buoys on the Shatt Al-Arab in the late thirties and the war years. One such character was a crewman on Matt's workboat. A heavy drinker, the man was reputed to satiate his craving for alcohol by filtering metal polish through a cloth and then drinking the filtrate which contained some alcohol. It was also claimed that he extracted the alcohol from French polish for the same purpose.

One day Matt found him in his bunk unable to speak or open his mouth. Apparently, he had drunk a bottle of varnish, believing it to be an alcoholic solution. The man's teeth were firmly cemented together by the varnish, and Matt and a crewman had to prise his teeth and jaws apart with a screwdriver wrapped in cloth.

Once his jaws were freed and with a shot of medicinal brandy under his belt the man returned to work as though nothing had happened. Matt commented that after this incident he had no more trouble with missing varnish, but still had to hide the metal polish!

In June 1956, I was due to go on leave. My preparations completed, I went over to the power station to say farewell to Pop Demain, the plant Superintendent, and his staff. In the reception area of the station, I was approached by a stranger who I had not seen before in Kuwait. Seeming to be lost and unsure of where he was going, I asked if I could be of assistance. 'Thank you,' he replied. He went on to say that he was visiting the Emirate for a few days on business and wanted to see the desalination plant before he returned to the UK.

He seemed to be a pleasant enough person, slim and distinguished looking, and was somewhat over medium height. Sporting a brown tweed suit and cream shirt and dark red spotted bow tie, he gave the impression of being an artist or writer. He was smoking a cigarette in a long amber holder in a No Smoking area. I had to ask him to put the cigarette out.

I suggested that he accompany me to meet the plant Superintendent and obtain permission to see the plant. I offered to show him around when he had obtained the necessary permission.

Pop Demain was pleased to see us. Extremely proud of the plant that had been designed by Ewbank and Partners, the consultancy firm who seconded him to the Kuwait government, he was always pleased to show people around his 'baby'. As I had expected Pop offered to accompany us on our tour.

The stranger explained that he had come to Kuwait to do some technical writing for the Kuwait Oil Company. He was in the process of preparing a manuscript for a book on various cities around the world and had just been to Japan, Hong Kong and

India. On his way back to the UK, he had taken the opportunity to call into Kuwait to complete his assignment with the Kuwait Oil Company.

The stranger, Pop and I left the office for our proposed tour of the station. Surprisingly, the stranger proved to be most interested in the plant and demonstrated an excellent grasp of the technical side of the desalination process. Pop blossomed in this atmosphere of genuine interest and went out of his way to answer all the stranger's questions in depth. The tour of the plant finally completed, Pop bade the stranger goodbye and wished me a safe and pleasant journey for the following day and a safe return.

The stranger had unwisely dismissed his taxi upon arriving at the power station. In June it is not advisable to be without transport. There is no pleasure, in fact it quickly becomes a traumatic experience, to stand out in the hot Kuwaiti sunshine trying to flag down passing taxis. I offered to take him back to his hotel.

The following day, Eric Jenkins kindly took me to the airport to catch the British Airways Constellation flight back to London. In those days, the Kuwait to London flight took a long eighteen hours with stops at Baghdad, Aman, Rome and Frankfurt.

When I actually boarded the plane, I found that I was seated next to the stranger of the previous day. I had not seen him in the airport waiting area and had forgotten that he would be travelling on the same plane to London. As a guest of the Kuwait Oil Company he would have stayed at their guest house before being taken to the airport in their official transport.

He seemed quite glad to see me, no doubt after all his travels he was pleased to see a friendly and familiar face.

The plane trundled down the sandy runway and

climbed reluctantly into the air, the maximum load of passengers, freight and fuel holding it earthbound until the last moment. Once airborne, the stranger proved to be a most entertaining companion. His in-depth knowledge covering a great variety of subjects ensured that our conversation didn't pall throughout the flight.

When we landed at Aman we had to leave the plane while it was refuelled. We passed the waiting time in watching various military aircraft landing and taking off in rapid sequence. Apparently, the airport also served as a military base. His depth of knowledge of military aircraft was surprising. When I questioned him on the subject he told me that during the war he had been in the navy and for a time had been involved in statistical studies of military aircraft.

My companion continued to help to pass the long flying hours pleasantly. Listening to him was so interesting that I almost regretted the end of the flight when the aircraft wheels touched down at Heathrow. As we said goodbye he gave me his card and asked me to look him up when next I was in London. The name on the card was Ian Fleming. I never did meet him again. At that time he was not famous, it was some time before his first James Bond book was published. Once home, I had little thought for anything but enjoying a few days vacation with my old friends and family.

7

Sailing

The Shuwaikh beach was also the location of the Kuwait Dolphin Yacht Club, a sailing club, which had been founded for their employees by a number of the major foreign companies operating in Kuwait. Each participating company had either donated a sailing dinghy for the use of club members or had contributed towards the construction of the club house and its amenities on the beach.

Although originally intended for the sole use of employees of the founding companies, the club membership had been opened to all foreign residents of Kuwait. At the time of my arrival in Kuwait, membership of the Club had become a status symbol, much sought after by all aspiring socialites amongst the expatriates. Because of the popularity of the Club, one had to be of considerable standing in the community, usually of either management or professional status, before the committee would consider an application for membership.

Shortly after my arrival, I was requested to become Honorary Secretary of the Yacht Club, an office that I was privileged to hold for over fifteen years. With hindsight, I have no delusions why I was asked to accept this office. No-one else was prepared to accept the considerable amount of work associated with the position! The job had many compensations. I met many interesting people and saw a number of facets to life that I would not have been party to otherwise.

At my first committee meeting, I was privileged to witness class snobbery at its worst. We were reviewing applications for membership when one particular gentleman's name came up for consideration. I knew him well! He was an engineer in the main workshop of the Shuwaikh Power & Desalination Plant, a decent person, who had a keen interest in sailing.

When the gentleman's name came up for consideration, the then Commodore of the Club, the Shuwaikh Port Captain, looked down his nose and said, 'I'm afraid that I don't know this chap! What is his social position in Kuwait?' When it was pointed out that the person in question was only a relatively junior power plant engineer, I, as Club Secretary, was directed to inform him that membership was full and that his name would be put on the 'Waiting List'.

I was to learn in those early days that few applicants for membership managed to escape the probing social status evaluation of the Commodore! To be assigned to the 'Waiting List' was tantamount to being sent to limbo for ever! This was one of the less attractive sides of social activities in Kuwait and one which I worked hard to change.

As Yacht Club Secretary from 1954 to 1970, I was aware of the various changes in membership that reflected the gradual change in the expatriate community as a whole. Gradually, the almost total preponderance of senior government and contractors' professional and management personnel and their wives gave way to technicians and semi-skilled personnel from Kuwaiti-owned organizations who were mainly employed on short term bachelor status contracts.

Sadly, these changes were not always for the better. With the advent of the short term, single status employee, interest in the development and long term growth of the Club gradually faded. In general, the more recent members were interested in maximizing their personal savings over the period of their short term contracts. They were reluctant to spend either time or money developing the Club for the benefit of other members.

In the early days, before these changes took place, the Dolphin Yacht Club was a hive of activity. In addition to the sailing and racing activities, the Social Committee of the Club arranged regular functions and entertainment for the members. These took the form of 'After Race Refreshment' comprising curry lunches and bar snacks and regular monthly social evenings and dances. Seasonal events in the form of Christmas, New Year and Easter parties were the highlight of the social calendar.

Curry lunches were served at the club house on Thursdays and Fridays, after racing. A large helping of blistering Madras curry, washed down by large quantities of cold beer, was sufficient to render even the most hardy sailor incapable of anything other than dozing the afternoon away in the shade of the boat shed, or alternatively, relaxing in the warm shallows along the beach. Less hardy members would slip off home after lunch to take their afternoon siesta in the cool, air conditioned seclusion of their own bedrooms.

Social evenings, complete with buffet dinner, were held at least twice each month. The House Committee would prepare and serve the food; a true labour of love! These meals were magnificent efforts and highly popular with the membership, particularly so in the warm balmy evenings from March to June and October to December. January and February were far too cold and July, August and September were too hot and humid to be pleasant.

At Christmas and New Year, parties were held for the children. Father Christmas never failed to appear. He would arrive by launch after being surreptitiously picked up some way down the beach, out of sight of the club house.

As the launch approached the shore, Father Christmas could be seen standing in the bows, waving to the excited children crowding on the beach to meet him. With his sack of toys over his shoulder, he would lead the group up the beach to the club house. Here a further complement of sacks containing sufficient toys for distribution to all the children awaited him.

He spoke to each child in turn, presenting them with a small gift and enquiring what they wanted most for Christmas. This would be entered laboriously in a red and gold bound notebook. The children loved this part of the ceremony and held long conversations with Father Christmas.

Finally, after a large glass of sherry, Father Christmas would embark on his launch, leaving the group of excited children standing on the beach, waving and calling after him as he sailed out of sight past the port jetty.

In later years, Father Christmas was played by Fred Smith, a tall, well-built man, with the general appearance and manner of a village policeman. On one particular occasion in the late sixties he arrived at the Yacht Club party by boat. He greeted the children and as he handed out their gifts he would ask each one what they would like for Christmas. It was his proud boast that no-one ever recognized him.

A week later he was invited to our home for dinner. As he came up the path our son, Tommy, ran out to meet him, 'Hello Uncle Fred,' he said. 'Have you brought my train with you?' Fred tried hard to brazen it out, but to no avail! He had been recognized.

The Sailing Section was always busy. Racing fixtures were held at weekends and holidays, while instruction and practice sails were held each afternoon. Whenever possible, visiting teams were invited to race at the Club. These events were looked forward to with great enthusiasm by all the racing members looking for new fields to conquer!

British Naval frigates on patrol in the Gulf to prevent piracy, slaving and gold smuggling, were regular callers at Kuwait. Their crews, always eager to escape the boredom of the ship's routine, would muster teams to sail against the Club. In the 1960s, the frigate HMS *Wren,* was our most popular sailing competitor. The crew members of the *Wren* were well known and popular. They were always eager to send a team ashore to sail against the Club.

At regular intervals regattas were arranged with the Cumberland Yacht Club and the Kuwait Oil Company Yacht Club. In the early days this club was located some two hundred metres along the beach from us. In later years they moved to the 'Small Boat Harbour' near Mina Al Ahmadi, the oil company's town. The oil company employees tended to look down on the Dolphin Yacht Club; not only did they consider themselves to be the senior club, but they sailed X-class keel boats, whereas the Dolphin Yacht Club only sailed Fireflies – small, moulded ply-wood dinghies!

Whenever the Cumberland Yacht Club crews visited Shuwaikh, the Dolphin Yacht Club took great delight in trouncing them soundly. Our small dinghies were difficult to sail in a good breeze, even for those used to their characteristics. Helmsmen used to sailing the larger, more forgiving, keel boats found the small dinghies to be a continuous source of trouble. Almost without exception, they would capsize two or three times during a race.

On the return match, it was a different story. Our lack of experience and technique in the large keel boats made us quite vulnerable. Although we did manage to win periodically, the Cumberland Yacht Club were usually the victors at these times.

The majority of expatriates had no previous sailing experience prior to joining the Club. Senior sailing members were appointed as instructors to teach the other members to sail safely, without constituting a danger either to themselves or to others.

After a period of instruction and a test of proficiency, the learner helmsman was given a Novices Certificate. This confirmed that he had a working knowledge of the RYC's Racing and Sailing Rules and could control a dinghy with a reasonable degree of safety. Later, with some instruction in the theory of navigation, he could sit for his Master Helmsman's Certificate.

Racing fever affected most helmsmen. Some were stimulated to excel themselves while others completely lost their heads. The pressure of competition made them forget all the simple basic procedures and rules that should have been second nature to them.

Harry, for example, was a professional maintenance engineer used to working under stress in his day-to-day job, yet many times in preparation for a race, he would omit to carry out even the most rudimentary of checks.

Often, under the stress of the moment, he would sail away from the shore to join the line-up of competitors waiting for the start of the race, only to find that he had forgotten to lower the rudder or replace the drain bungs in the transom.

Unable to steer, he would bear down on the other competitors completely out of control. His rudder thrashed wildly in the air as he moved the helm from side to side in a desperate attempt to steer the boat, waving in panic at the other dinghies to get out of his way. The other helmsmen shouted appropriate derogatory remarks at him as they took evasive action to avoid his uncontrolled advance across their course.

On other occasions, Harry would forget to replace the drain plugs in the rear transom. He would sail gaily away from the shore, gradually sinking lower in the sea as the boat filled with water. Finally, with the boat completely waterlogged, he would desperately resort to bailing in an attempt to stem the inrushing water. With the drain plugs still missing this was a losing battle. When he at last realized this, he would sit despondently in the rising water, watching the race start without him; his dinghy gradually sinking lower and lower, until finally the buoyancy bags prevented it foundering completely.

In other instances, race fever turned mild, kindly people into unconscionable monsters. At such times they were prepared to sacrifice their crew or rival the helmsman without compunction should it serve their purpose.

Hans was such a person! A charming, considerate, mild-mannered man on land, he would change completely once he was in his dinghy with a race in the offing. This helpful little man would blossom into the

Captain Bligh of Kuwait Bay!

One particularly breezy race day, Hans was leading the pack in a race around the first marker buoy. A sudden gust of wind caused his dinghy to keel over. His crewman, caught unawares, fell overboard! Hans was loath to lose his lead in the race, but dutifully went about to pick up the unfortunate man from the water.

As he retraced his course to rescue his companion, the other boats shot past him. Their triumphant helmsmen waving in derision! This was too much for his Captain Bligh libido that lurked somewhere in his subconscious. Before his unfortunate crewman could climb back on board, Hans was back on course trying to regain his position in the race.

His unfortunate crew member was left behind waving frantically. The Commodore's launch was forced to rush to pick him up before a hungry shark arrived at the scene! It is not surprising that after this incident Hans had great difficulty in raising a crew.

Midweek a group of ladies used the Club for their morning Coffee Meetings. It was common knowledge that little or no coffee was drunk at these affairs, they were an excuse for the ladies to get together for a quiet drink, a game of cards and an exchange of local gossip. As Club Secretary, I had to visit the Club at odd times during the mornings. Sometimes my visits coincided with one of the coffee parties.

At such times I was always made most welcome, particularly so when the ladies had a point to make regarding the Club or its members. Coffee was never available, only gin, whisky, wines and local soft drinks. As a non-drinker, I would satisfy my thirst with a Coke, while the ladies, who did not have a job to return to, floated around on a hazy, warm cloud of pink gin.

The ladies were, in general, elderly matrons whose husbands were in senior positions in the Kuwait Government Service, or associated with the oil company. Many had lived for most of their lives in India, where their husbands had either been in the army or civil service. Their comments and opinions usually carried considerable weight in the local expatriate politics. Consequently, it was always useful to hear their complaints and comments at first hand, prior to official publication in the form of a letter from their husbands to the committee.

One particular day, I had gone to the Club to collect some papers. The ladies, as usual, were sitting around in their swimsuits, sipping pink gins and discussing the latest scandals amongst the membership in general. One particular lady was emphasizing a point by vigorously waving her arms. As she raised her arms with even more energy, a large breast popped out of her costume. Quickly, I looked away, hoping not to embarrass her.

After a respectable period I returned my gaze to the group, expecting that the offending member would have been neatly stowed back in place. This was not the case! Her conversation was continuing without interruption, her breast swinging freely with each gesture.

I averted my eyes once again, this time for a longer period before glancing back. It was still there, drawing my eyes like a magnet. Suddenly, with another wild swing of her arm, her other breast fell out to join its companion on display. I felt an almost uncontrollable desire to laugh. I kept thinking of a comment of a friend when placed in a similar situation. He said that he had stepped forward like a gentleman with two warm spoons to correct the situation.

She finally appeared to notice the disarray of her anatomy, and quite casually tucked her breasts back into the confines of her loose swimsuit top. I made my excuses and left quickly! It was apparent from the casual attitude of the ladies to this situation, that such instances were by no means uncommon. I could not have faced another similar exposure without losing all self-control and bursting into uncontrollable laughter.

One Friday morning, some weeks later, I went to the Club only to find a large group of members standing around on the beach watching a recent member floundering around in the water close to the beach, with a hose pipe in his mouth. As a Club official, I thought it my duty to find out whether he was trying to commit suicide, had been overcome by the sun or was simply practising scuba diving. As I drew near I recognized him as a quantity surveyor who had recently come to Kuwait along with his American wife, Eleanor. As I approached, he looked up and said, 'Would you mind putting your foot on my back to keep me down?' When I asked him what he was trying to do, he explained, 'I am trying to find Eleanor's false teeth. She lost them while swimming earlier this morning!' I suggested that it was a hopeless task and dangerous into the bargain. He snorted in disgust, 'If you saw Eleanor without her teeth you would know how important it is to find them.'

Obligingly, bowing to his dire need to recover the teeth, I held him down with my foot until his random groping along the sandy bottom turned into a wild scrabbling at my leg. I interpreted this as a signal that he wished to surface and removed my foot from his back. He emerged from the depths red faced and gasping, 'You're right,' he said, 'it's hopeless!'

As soon as he had regained his breath he began to bemoan the loss of Eleanor's teeth. We tried to comfort him by telling him that he could have a new set made within a few days at the dental department of the Amerie Hospital, but to no avail. Apparently, they were going out to dinner that evening and he felt it imperative that she have her teeth. In actual fact, Eleanor was quite an attractive girl and his criticism was really quite unfair.

That same evening, we met again at the dinner party. Eleanor hardly spoke and when she did, it was with considerable difficulty. She didn't eat anything, although it appeared that she had found her teeth, which appeared to be considerably worse for wear after their enforced immersion in the sea water. Her teeth were misshapen and a particularly strange grey colour. Later, I spoke to her husband and complimented him upon his persistence in finding her teeth.

To my surprise he said he hadn't found them. After a fruitless afternoon of searching, he had gone home and made Eleanor a set of teeth out of candle wax! No wonder the teeth looked strange and Eleanor could not eat. She must have loved him a great deal to put up with it all!

Fortunately, the story had a happy ending. Some days later Ali, The Boatman, found the teeth in the sand. Needless to say, both Eleanor and her husband were delighted to have the teeth back once more.

The scourge of the Kuwait beaches was the stone fish, an ugly creature with the appearance of a piece of encrusted rock. Dangerous as it is ugly, the stone fish is armed with a series of dorsal spines which inject a virulent and sometimes lethal venom upon contact. The fish secrets itself between stones and pieces of dead coral, preying upon small fish and shrimps which are unfortunate enough to stray within reach of its ugly mouth.

The sluggish creature is not aggressive, but its torpid nature and reluctance to move away when disturbed, together with its excellent camouflage make a ready trap for an unwary bather's foot. To be stung by a stone fish is an extremely painful and dangerous experience. Unless he receives immediate medical attention, the victim's life is in grave danger.

Because of the ever present danger of stone fish along the beaches in the Gulf, swimmers and yachtsmen are always advised to wear tough soled shoes whenever they walk or wade in the shallow water along the shoreline. The sailing club regularly organized Stone Fish Clearing Parties. At low tide a group of volunteers armed with sharp rods or fishing spears and a bucket, would gather on the beach. By prodding each stone-like object in the shallow water, it was possible to collect a large number of stone fish before the rising tide put an end to the hunt. When a fish was speared, it would make a loud, hoarse croaking noise as it was pulled out of the water and placed in the bucket. Great care had to be taken, as even in death the poisonous spines on its back were still deadly.

One day in late summer, an English family and their ten-year-old daughter were on the beach. The daughter had just been learning to sail. Upon returning to the beach, she leapt out of the dinghy into the shallow water and jumped a little, saying that she had pricked her foot on a stone. Within a few seconds she started to cry, saying that her foot was burning. I carried her up the beach to her mother, but by the time we had covered the 150 metres her foot and ankle had swollen considerably.

Guessing what had happened, I carried on up the

92

beach to my car and drove as fast as possible to the nearest hospital. By the time we reached the emergency treatment department not more than fifteen minutes had elapsed. Yet in that short time she was in deep shock and her whole leg had swollen into an angry-looking tube of flesh.

The medical staff knew exactly what action to take and they injected antihistamine and antitoxin directly into the area of the sting. By the time her parents arrived at the hospital she was fairly comfortable but extremely poorly. Once out of danger, it took six weeks of convalescing before she was back to her normal self. This incident impressed everyone at the Club with the importance of wearing beach shoes in the water.

There were many other unpleasant creatures inhabiting the warm, beckoning waters of the Arabian Gulf. Not least of these was the stingray. These creatures, which grow to a considerable size, carry a long thorn-like barb on their horny tails. If one was unfortunate enough to be struck by one of them, an extremely painful and slow healing wound resulted.

Not too long ago, the slave traders of the Arabian Gulf and Red Sea coasts carried whips made out of the tails of large stingrays. It is doubtful that they were ever used, because the damage such a weapon would cause to their valuable properties would be enormous. No doubt the threat of a lashing with such a fearsome instrument was enough to subjugate even the most defiant of captives.

Another unpleasant inhabitant of the Arabian Gulf was the sea snake. During the hot, still summer afternoons, when the surface of the sea is like a burnished mirror, sea snakes can often be seen sunning themselves on the surface. Although their poison is more virulent than that of a cobra, it is fortunate that their mouths are not large enough to pose a major threat to swimmers and bathers.

My first contact with a sea snake occurred sailing on Kuwait Bay. As the breeze was quite strong, I was riding well out over the thwart with my feet under the toe straps. Suddenly, I felt something lash against my back. Glancing over my shoulder, I saw a large sea snake racing away across the surface of the sea. It must have been dozing on the surface, and was taken completely unaware as I struck him with my backside. Fortunately, the snake was as surprised as I was and only thought of flight. It was large enough to have bitten me, were it so minded.

My second encounter with sea snakes was some years later. I was then married and we were living at Salmiyah, to the south of Kuwait City. Our son, then aged six, had been on the beach with some friends. They returned to the flat carrying a small beach bucket, which contained eight, highly venomous sea snakes. They had picked the snakes out of the shallows by the beach with their bare hands!

After some deliberation, I decided that the only thing to do was to shoot them and flush them down the toilet. This was done with haste, much to the chagrin of the boys who had hopes of keeping the poisonous creatures as pets!

8

The Shuwaikh Social Club

In the early years, the Shuwaikh Club was the centre of social activities for the expatriate population of Kuwait City.

The oil company had its own social amenities. They included the Hubara Club, a palatial building when compared with the Shuwaikh Club, and possessing every possible amenity imaginable. The Kuwait Oil Company employees also enjoyed the use of a number of other clubs including: a power boat club; the Yacht Club, whose membership comprised the elite of the company's employees, or so was the general belief amongst the staff, a motoring club which held regular desert car rallies; and a small golf course which was the envy of the Kuwait City expatriates. These amenities were jealously guarded by the oil company employees; for a Kuwait City expatriate to be invited to share them was honour indeed.

Government employees, contractors' people and the employees of Kuwaiti businesses all used the Shuwaikh Club as the focal point of their social life. The club was managed by a committee comprising a cross section of the camp residents, government employees and contractors' personnel.

The committee managed the day-to-day running of the Club under the close surveillance of Angus McDonald, the Camp Manager, and his staff. Angus's presence on the committee ensured that Kuwait Government interests were protected and things did not get too far out of hand. There were always a number of madcaps amongst the contractors' personnel who, for sheer devilment, were prepared to propose all sorts of wild schemes to the committee!

Ricky Williams, the Club Chairman, was the head of the design section of the Ministry of Public Works. He was a large, bald and extremely overweight gentleman. Both he and his wife, Peggy, were typical 'club people'. Their whole social life centred around the Club bar and its clientele.

As head of the architectural design section of the Ministry of Public Works, Ricky was quite an important person. His position in the Government Service justified an official car, a large black Humber saloon, complete with chauffeur. Ricky himself did not like to drive, being extremely nervous on the road even when he was not behind the wheel. Consequently, whenever he was out in the car, a mandatory speed limit of thirty kilometres per hour was enforced upon his driver.

It was a common sight in those early days to see Ricky and Peggy driving sedately through the crowded streets of downtown Kuwait in their large black Humber saloon car. Their regal progress through the town was always at the head of a long procession of protesting cars which were manned by frustrated, fuming drivers. They sounded their horns continuously and waved their free arms out of their windows with all the emphasis and meaning that only an irate Arab driver is capable of expressing.

Their fruitless efforts to pass the Williams's car in the crowded streets were blissfully ignored by Ricky's immaculately uniformed chauffeur. Completely oblivious to the chaos and cacophony following in their wake, Peggy and Ricky sailed regally along towards their destination. Their habit of driving in this cermonial manner to the Club earned them the title 'The Lord Mayor and Lady Mayoress of Shuwaikh', a title which stuck with them to their final departure from Kuwait in the early sixties.

Ricky and Peggy were both gregarious, extroverted people. After working hours, they could always be found in the Club bar. Their intake of alcohol was prodigious and although they floated through those early Kuwait days on a mist of pink gins and dry martinis, they never appeared to be the worse for drink. They were always courteous and polite, prepared to chat with anyone willing to join them at the bar.

One evening, Peggy left the Club after a slight disagreement with Ricky. In some degree of pique she insisted on walking home herself. Unfortunately, in her hurry to depart she had forgotten that Ricky still had the house key. When she arrived at the house the door was locked and she couldn't gain entrance as their houseboy was away at the cinema. Peggy was not one to be upset by trifles. She sat for a while on the balcony, but beginning to feel sleepy as the warmth of the night and the alcohol took effect, she lay down on a rug by the front door to await Ricky's return. Within a few minutes she was fast asleep.

Shortly afterwards, the houseboy returned from the camp cinema, where he had been to see an Indian film with his friends. The shock of finding his mistress lying apparently lifeless by the front door was too much for him. Without bothering to investigate further, he ran as fast as he could to the Club to find Ricky. There, with some difficulty, he was able to gain Ricky's attention and impart the sad news that Peggy had inadvertently passed away.

Ricky showed amazing resourcefulness and control. After a couple of large whiskys to steady his nerves, he called upon the assistance of a doctor who happened to be present in the bar at the time. With a couple of more drinks under their belts to shore up their nerves for the ordeal ahead of them, they left for Ricky's house.

By this time, the sad news had circulated throughout the bar. Consequently, when Ricky and the doctor finally left the Club, they were followed by many of the other members who had become party to the tragic news.

Arriving at the house, they stood respectfully to one side while the doctor began to examine Peggy's remains. 'She appears to have had a coronary,' he said to all in general. 'Probably brought on by walking in the heat! She can't have been dead long. The body is still quite warm and there is no sign of rigidity,' he said, prodding Peggy vigorously. He leapt back with an exclamation, as Peggy belched loudly and gave a yawn then stretched, turned on her side and fell fast asleep again, snoring loudly.

There was a prodigious silence! The doctor shuffled his feet in embarrassment, muttering something about poor light and bad information. Ricky was the first to stir. He looked down at Peggy in obvious relief then went into the house emerging with a pillow and a blanket. He carefully placed the pillow under Peggy's head and covered her with the blanket.

After completing these niceties, a token of his affection for her, he invited the doctor and all interested bystanders back to the Club for a drink to celebrate the fact that Peggy was indeed alive and well. Later, when Peggy was told of the events of the evening, she said that it was disgraceful that they had not awakened her, in order that she could have joined them in the celebrations!

It was a general custom at the time for married ladies to take turns in hosting a weekly coffee morning. On such a morning, the ladies would arrive at the hostess's home around 10.00 a.m. They would sip coffee, nibble canapés and exchange local gossip until around noon, when their drivers would arrive to take them home in time for their husbands' return from the office. Then, armed with the latest gossip of the morning, they would regale their spouse with all the news and scandal involving his workmates and their families!

Peggy's coffee mornings were slightly different. Once her guests were assembled and seated, Peggy would appear with a drinks trolley. 'Anyone wanting coffee can go and make it!' she would say, and would then proceed to serve everyone with numerous large pink gins.

Whenever a glass was emptied it was immediately refilled. Peggy was always over-generous in her hospitality! It wasn't uncommon, after such a coffee morning, for many of her guests to be in need of assistance to walk to their cars.

The more moderate drinkers amongst the ladies tended to avoid Peggy's coffee mornings like the plague, but the hard liners looked forward to these 'At Homes', as she called them, with considerable relish. The husbands of these particular ladies usually planned the day well in advance. On Peggy's At Home days the majority of them took their lunch in the bachelor mess at the Shuwaikh Camp; well knowing they would receive short shrift at home. The more knowledgeable and experienced among them even took dinner at the mess as well. Discretion being the better part of valour, experience told them that after the morning session at Peggy's, it would be at least a couple of days before their spouse would be sufficiently recovered to prepare a decent meal for them.

The Ministry of Public Works, where Ricky worked, had recently completed construction of a new sand-lime brick plant to manufacture kiln cured bricks made from a mixture of local sand and lime. The latter being produced by burning the local coral limestone in a large rotary kiln. The plant was destined to be beset by teething problems.

Initially, the boiler exploded. The gas-fired furnace inadvertently went out and before the furnace could be purged of gas by blowing air through it, someone attempted to light the fire once again. They were too successful! The boiler exploded and shot forward like a rocket, destroying part of the boiler house and a workshop in the process. Fortunately, no-one was hurt, but the start-up of the plant was delayed while repairs were carried out.

A recent arrival at the camp was the gentleman recruited as the kiln manager or lime burner. Because of the problem at the plant, his services were not required for some time. As a result, he joined Les Doe and Dan McGraw as one more highly paid gentleman of leisure.

Shortly after his arrival, it became rumoured that the gentleman in question was a 'remittance man'. That is to say that he was a man from a good family who had in some way disgraced his family name. In order to keep him out of the way and providing that he stayed out of the country, away from his family and their friends, the family remitted a sum of money each month to him.

He proved to be a man of many talents, but in spite of his many capabilities, he turned out to be a liability both to himself and his friends. Somehow, he managed to impress the Ministry of Public Works of his capabilities, convincing them that he possessed unique skills in the field of lime burning. He certainly possessed skills, of that there was no doubt, but not in the context implied.

His position carried an excellent salary grade. This together with his unstinting praise of his own capabilities and professional prowess, he claimed to be one of the world's leading authorities· in the lime burning field, soon earned him a position in the local social hierarchy.

His successful campaign of self-promotion soon gained him rapid entry into the social whirl of the upper strata of the expatriate community. Within a short time, Don, as he was called, became a regular guest at Embassy functions. He became a personal friend of the Political Agent himself, and was sought after as a guest at all the major social gatherings in Kuwait's expatriate society.

Don was a surprisingly complex person to say the least! He was a homosexual, an alcoholic and a contortionist to boot, amongst his many accomplishments.

Shortly after his arrival in Kuwait, Don developed a preference for dressing in Arab clothing; whether he thought this would impress the Kuwaitis, or that he simply wished to foster the impression of his already eccentric character, is difficult to say. Nevertheless, he would wander around in his *dishdasha* or *thobe,* the long white garment worn by the Arab men. Whenever he attended parties or receptions, he would appear wearing full Arab dress. On such occasions, he would arrive wearing a beautiful, gold trimmed *bisht* the long, embroidered cloak made from finely spun goat or camel hair, which was usually only worn by the wealthy Arabs on formal occasions.

At the time, the Sand-Lime Brick Plant was not yet operational. Consequently, Don had plenty of free time on his hands. Most of this was spent in the Club bar with his cronies. Lunch for him was a half bottle of champagne mixed with half a bottle of brandy. Mixed, not stirred, and drunk from a champagne glass!

It was his practice to take his 'lunch' dressed in his *dishdasha*. He would sit perched on the bar with one leg curled over his shoulder from the rear, like the contortionist he certainly was. A champagne glass would be held between the toes of his free foot with which he would raise the glass to his lips at regular intervals. A cigarette would be held in the fingers of one hand, while he gesticulated with his free hand to emphasize any point he was making in his conversation.

Don's presence in the bar always ensured an audience. As a consequence, bar sales increased considerably at lunch times and in the evenings when he held court there. This was much to the delight of the Entertainments Committee who utilized the income from bar sales to finance other Club activities.

For a short period of time Don was my neighbour in the Shuwaikh Camp. His neighbour on the other side was Hamie Milne, the Water Engineer, a quiet, gentle person who would never say or do anything to embarrass or hurt anyone. Hamie had been Assistant Water Engineer in Singapore. During the early part of World War Two, prior to the Japanese occupation of Singapore, he had been imprisoned in Changhi Jail by the Japanese because he would not collaborate with them and like so many others, he was badly treated and tortured. His experiences in the Japanese concentration camp left him with an undying fear and hatred of the Japanese. He could not sit in the same room with a Japanese without feeling physically sick. He also suffered from terrible recurring nightmares of the camp and the atrocities he had witnessed.

Don's heavy drinking was not without price. He would periodically suffer from hallucinations. At such times, using different voices, he would hold lengthy conversations with himself. He would argue, shout, laugh and joke with himself, depending upon his mood at the time. At times it sounded as though his room was full of people, although we knew only Don was there. Sometimes he would throw furniture around and rattle the fly netting at his windows. As all this activity mainly occurred at night, it was annoying to say the least.

Unfortunately, the loud noises and commotion in the early hours would often trigger one of Hamie's nightmares. He would wake with a start, sweating in fear and expecting the Japanese camp guard to appear at any moment. Consequently, he could not get back to sleep and after a while of fruitlessly trying, he would get up, dress and knock on my door for a little company and hopefully, a cup of tea. We would then chat, sipping our tea and wait patiently until Don finally settled down for the night, before returning to our own beds.

As Don's consumption of champagne and brandy increased, his bouts of nocturnal ranting occurred more frequently. One particular night the block was awakened by loud screams from the toilets. Everyone rushed out of their rooms to investigate in case someone was in serious trouble. We found Don standing completely naked in the middle of the

103

bathroom floor, his clothes scattered around him. He was screaming and shouting, frantically brushing imaginary insects off his body. He claimed that he could see and feel huge black beetles crawling all over him.

Despite all our efforts, it wasn't possible to pacify him and finally we had to send for medical help. The doctor gave him an injection to tranquillize him and then dispatched him to the hospital for further treatment.

After seeing this lurid example of the DTs, many of the Club's hardened drinkers drastically reduced their consumption of alcohol. It's one thing to laugh and joke about the DTs and friendly visitations of pink elephants, rabbits etc. but quite another to see the stark horror and terror generated by real hallucinations.

The British Embassy, for reasons of security, had appointed local wardens. These were responsible people, each assigned to a specific district. It was their responsibility to liaise between the Embassy and the local expatriates in time of any possible civil emergency. The wardens were provided with a portable radio for communication with the Embassy on a scheduled basis.

Don, for some inexplicable reason, had been selected by the Embassy as the 'responsible person' in the Shuwaikh area. It was not particularly reassuring, to be aware that possibly one's safety and even one's life, might be in the hands of the local dipsomaniac.

Nevertheless, the appointment had been made and we could do nothing about it. Therefore there was a considerable sense of poetic justice amongst the members of the Camp, when during the night Don would switch on the radio linking him to the Embassy and deliver a tirade of vituperation and abuse to the official on night duty. He used his various voices and held three-sided conversations amongst himself, his alto-ego and the Embassy radio operator. As he never identified himself, they were not able to discover who the culprit was, and as Don had little or no daytime recollection of his nightly broadcasts, he appeared to be completely innocent, joining enthusiastically in the Embassy's indignant search for the offender.

Fortunately, for the well-being of both Hamie Milne and the Embassy radio operators, Don was finally dismissed from the employ of the Sand-Lime Brick Plant. A combination of circumstances and his reputation for heavy drinking finally persuaded the management at the plant to terminate his employment with them.

The circumstances involved a problem at the official opening of the plant. Once the boiler was replaced, the Sand-Lime Brick Plant was required to be fully operational at the time of the scheduled grand opening. Consequently, it was necessary to import lime from overseas in order to charge the huge lime storage silo prior to starting the plant.

It was a painstaking process. Under Don's direction, the bags of lime had to be carried up to the top of the silo and emptied into its cavernous storage space. This tedious operation was finally completed the day prior to the opening, much to the relief of the management.

The great day arrived! The Sheikhs and local dignitaries lined up, the speeches were made and the Sheikh stepped forward and pressed the button to start the process. The silo door opened, and nothing happened! A measured quantity of lime should have fallen onto the conveyor. The button was pressed again and again but to no avail. Finally, in deep chagrin, the

Board of Directors had to apologize to the Sheikh and the dignitaries. As soon as the guests had left the site, a major investigation was begun.

Many theories were propounded as to the reason why the lime did not flow from the silo. Some suggested that the silo was empty, others that high humidity had caused the lime to solidify, but none was correct. It was finally discovered that the silo was full of lime, but in bags! Instead of being full to the brim with loose-powdered lime ready to pour evenly from the base as soon as the discharge gate was opened, the silo was found to contain neatly packed double-wall-thickness paper bags of lime! No-one had informed the labourers carrying the bags to the top of the silo that they should empty the bags, they had simply dropped them into it.

Someone had to carry the blame for this fiasco, and as Don's other problems had already reached the ears of management, the scales were already weighted against him, he was dismissed as quickly as protocol would allow.

Don's departure solved Hamie's sleeping problem. This provided the added bonus that I too could sleep at nights; without being awakened in the early hours by Hamie knocking at the door for his cup of tea.

Don did not immediately leave the country. He had become friendly with a British insurance agent employed in the private sector who managed to find him a job in a local company. He only held the position for a short while. His homosexual activities brought him into contact with the law and he was finally requested to leave the country.

Unlike Don, his friend was a rather scruffy individual. He had a predilection for dressing in red flannel trousers and a dirty, crumpled shirt with the collar awry, and open-toed Arab style sandals. He prided himself on his ability to compose poetry on any subject at a moment's notice. Sadly his poems were neither good poetry, nor in the best of taste. Few people liked him, but all felt sorry for his two children. They were always to be found in the rear of his Ford Thunderbird at all times of the day or night.

With such exceptions, the majority of Club members were decent hardworking people. Many of the residents of the camp had families at home and missed them considerably. They were always extremely grateful for the hospitality shown to them by the few families resident in Kuwait. The majority went out of their way to repay this kindness whenever the opportunity presented itself.

Christmas was such a time. The camp residents organized children's parties, and adult carnival dances throughout the Christmas and New Year period. The children's Christmas party always involved a real live Father Christmas complete with a dramatic entrance. One year at the Shuwaikh Club he arrived by helicopter, another year he was lowered down a specially constructed chimney to appear in a huge baronial fireplace specially erected for the occasion by the camp residents. At the Yacht Club, Father Christmas always arrived and departed by boat.

We all took turns at playing Father Christmas, some with more success than others. The more active members of the camp who participated in the school sports activities were easily recognized by the children. The lesser known members, such as myself, would be the subject of considerable guessing and conjecture for days after the party.

The highlight of the season was the New Year's Eve party. It was a truly magnificent affair, and all the expatriate community in Kuwait attended. When it came time to let out the 'Old Year' and herald in 'The New', it was traditional to have Ted Gowan, a tall, cadaverous-looking gentleman, dressed in a night shirt conveniently borrowed from the hospital, to represent the 'Old Year'. Ted would walk slowly around the hall carrying a large scythe and an hourglass. He made a perfect Father Time.

Close upon Ted's heels came Jack McLardie pushing a huge baby carriage containing Bill Gordon, a large man of over 130 kilos in weight and standing well over six feet in height. Bill was dressed in a baby bonnet and a huge nappy fastened with a massive safety pin. He held a large feeding bottle in one hand and in the other, a rattle. Each year, this group paraded ceremoniously around the hall welcoming in the New Year.

Needless to say, these parties were the highlight of the Club's social calendar; everyone unwound and had a great time. Yet, in spite of the distance away from home, the availability of liquor at unbelievable prices, the trying heat and the many pressures involved in working in the hostile desert environment, there were rarely problems in the way of fights or major altercations to disrupt the party atmosphere. There were many odd, eccentric people amongst the expatriates at that time, but they were neither mean nor aggressive in their nature.

Flash Calendar was a typical case in point. A member of a notable British industrial family, at the time in question he was employed by a firm of consulting engineers on the power station project. Flash was always a perfect gentleman. At all times he dressed immaculately in suit and tie. No matter how hot it was or how long he had been out in the heat of the day, he wore a coat and tie. His shirt was always spotless, looking as though he had just put it on. Although only employed in a relatively junior position, he exuded a slightly superior air, emphasized by his public school accent.

Flash was a compulsive photographer. Wherever he went he took photographs in large quantities. In order to ensure their success he always used a flash, hence his nickname. He had a most annoying habit of disposing of his used flash bulbs by slipping them into a convenient pocket of any unsuspecting person around him! It was not unusual to leave the dance floor during a Club dance to find one's pockets awash with burnt out flash bulbs. Flash had struck again!

9

Sharks And Other Fish

Bert Pashley was a civil engineer employed by the British Bank of the Middle East to supervise their building maintenance and development programmes. He and his family were enthusiastic members of the Sailing Club. Bert spent all his free time sailing and fishing in their boat, a small aluminium dinghy powered by an outboard engine. His wife and teenage daughter spent their time swimming and sunbathing on the beach while Bert sailed.

Bert's work with the bank took him all around the Gulf visiting various branches to carry out inspections of the buildings, arrange repairs and recommend modifications to the facilities. Shortly after his arrival in Kuwait, Bert was required to visit Khorfakhan in Fujera, a small Sheikhdom, surrounded to the north, south and west by the Sultanate of Oman and the sea to the east. In the early 1950s it was almost impossible to obtain a permit to enter or transit Oman, which at that time was a most inhospitable country. Consequently, the only practical access to Fujera was from the sea by boat.

Bert's trip required that he travel from Kuwait to Dubai by air, then, as at that time there were no roads across the mountains, by dhow from Dubai through the straits of Omuz to Fujera.

Bert was met at the Dubai Airport by the local bank representative who drove him directly to the dhow, which was about to sail from its moorings in the Dubai Creek. Being aware of the usual condition of the dhows which plied up and down the Gulf, Bert was amazed at the efficiency of the crew and the cleanliness of the quarters on the ramshackle-looking boat. He was even more surprised when, upon leaving the mouth of Dubai Creek, the dhow accelerated until it was cruising at a speed that would not have shamed a torpedo boat!

His surprise turned to alarm when, once out of sight of land, the hatches were opened and an amazing assortment of arms were unpacked. A heavy machine gun was mounted on the hatch and automatic weapons were issued to the crew. Even Bert was offered an automatic pistol which he immediately refused.

Initially, Bert had visions of being the object of a kidnap plot. The Captain sensing Bert's concern went to great lengths to put his mind at rest. He explained that to reach their destination, they had to sail around the 'Pirate Coast' of Musandam and North Oman. Piracy was still the order of the day along this section of the coast. Many dhows were involved in the gold smuggling trade between India and Dubai. The pirates considered these ships to be fair game. Whenever a rich prize was known to have sailed from Dubai *en route* for India, the pirates, who lived in the tiny coastal villages in this area, sailed forth to plunder the ship and murder the crew. The Captain explained that the pirates had an extremely efficient intelligence system and were able to obtain the sailing schedules of the gold smugglers' dhows.

111

The pirates would attempt to intercept the richer of the smugglers' vessels. Unless the smugglers could either out-run the pirates with their powerful engine and high speed craft, or fight them off by means of superior arms, the pirates would capture the smugglers' dhow. They would steal the cargo, murder the crew to a man and sink the ship, thus destroying all evidence of their crime. The ship would become a statistic, another vessel lost at sea without trace.

The Captain explained that this particular boat was owned by a powerful Dubai merchant. From time to time it carried sensitive cargo between Dubai and India. He did not specify what was meant by sensitive cargo, but Bert assumed that he was on a ship used for gold smuggling. The Captain went on to assure him that his ship was so fast and powerful, and the crew so well armed, that they were quite secure against any attack by pirates. Bert learnt later that his passage had been arranged on this particular boat for this specific reason. Nonetheless, he was quite relieved to reach Fujera safely and without incident.

Bert was an enthustiastic fisherman. In fact his only interests appeared to be fishing, beer and family in that order! He liked nothing better than to settle his wife and daughter on the beach at the Yacht Club. Then, with his family responsibilities completed, he would embark on a day's fishing with a couple of friends, two or three cartons of beer and a pack of sandwiches.

Bert was a most unlikely outdoor person! His complexion was extremely fair with ginger coloured hair, little or no skin pigmentation and freckles. Consequently, he suffered continuously from sunburn. Even a minimum amount of exposure to the sun's rays burnt his skin to an angry red. To counter this problem, his dress for the beach comprised baggy knee-length shorts, nondescript, long-sleeved shirts and a white floppy hat that had seen better days.

Friday was the most important day of the week for Bert and his cronies, Bob Rice of the US Embassy and one or another of his friends from the 'Bird Bank', the local nickname for the Kuwait Commercial Bank, because the senior four expatriates on the staff of the bank were named Raven, Wren, Sparrow and Hawk.

The trio would climb aboard Bert's dinghy, and sail eastward, parallel to the coast until they reached the Ras Al-Arhd, a headland at the mouth of Kuwait Bay. A number of strong tidal currents meeting by this headland formed an area of turbulence known as the Rhuksar.

The area was avoided by the Kuwait fishermen because of the dangerous tidal races that formed at certain states of the tide. It was also reputed to be the haunt of large sharks which came to feed upon the flotsam carried there by the currents. In spite of these hazards, it was also known as an excellent fishing area, hence Bert's interest.

One particular Friday, Bert and his friends were fishing at the Rhuksar as usual. Suddenly, they noticed a number of straw baskets in the distance. They were floating on the water and apparently drifting with the tide. Out of curiosity they sailed over to investigate, only to find that they contained offal from the local slaughter house. After spending some time in the sun the contents of the baskets had started to decompose and the smell was horrendous. Bert and his friends beat a hasty retreat and resumed their fishing.

Sometime later, Bert noted that there were fewer baskets floating in the sea than he remembered. He mentioned this to his companions and as they watched, one of the remaining baskets suddenly disappeared.

Starting the engine, they sailed over to investigate. As they arrived at the nearest basket, a huge shark, at least six metres in length, rose out of the water, opened its cavernous mouth and grasped a complete basket. The shark and the basket disappeared into the depths.

Bert and his friends sat paralyzed for the moment. Bob Rice was the first to recover. He snatched up his fishing line. 'Let's catch it!' he said, and began baiting his largest hook with lumps of raw fish from the bait box.

Suddenly, the shark reappeared, obviously to take another basket in a similar manner as before, but this time, before disappearing into the depths with its prize, the shark swam close under the boat. It actually scraped along the keel, rocking the boat as it swam beneath it. Bert looked over the side in time to gaze straight into the eye of the shark. He said later that it was black and expressionless, as large as the eye of a cow and looking directly at him. He said that he was never so frightened in his life!

The shark was considerably longer than Bert's boat, an aluminium skiff some four metres long with a reinforced transom to accept an outboard motor. Loaded as it was with three people, fuel and large quantities of beer, the boat had only some thirty centimetres of free board. The shark could easily have swamped the boat or turned it over. Some three kilometres from the coast and without buoyancy tanks they would not have had a chance in the water.

Bob Rice was undaunted! He tossed his line overboard, saying he would catch the shark if it was the last thing he did. This galvanized Bert to immediate action. He started the engine, turned the boat towards the coast and opened the throttle wide. He pulled out his sheath knife and laid it on the seat next to him in readiness. The thought of having that shark attached to his boat by even Bob Rice's thin fishing line was too frightful to contemplate. He was prepared to sever the line at the first indication of a bite.

In spite of Bob's complaints and demands to return to catch the shark, they reached the coast without incident. Bert then sailed in the shallowest possible water until they once again reached the Yacht Club. Bert said afterwards he believed that had the shark not been detracted away by the baskets of offal, it might well have attacked the boat. Had that occurred, they would have joined the ranks of other people mysteriously lost in the area of the Rhuksar.

It was many weeks before Bert would go fishing; although he braved the deep waters again, he always stayed clear of the Rhuksar area. He jokingly said that after their eyeball to eyeball contact, the shark would surely recognize him again if they met.

Some time later when Bert had recovered from this experience and had returned to his normal fishing activities, he promised Lilian, his wife, that he would bring some fish back for an evening meal. Confident in his fishing prowess he had invited a number of friends back for a traditional fish and chip supper. The presence of an unknown species in his catch, prompted him to check whether or not the various species of fish he had caught were suitable for the table. As Ali, the Club Boatman, was helping him to pull the skiff out of the water, Bert asked him, 'Can you eat these fish, Ali?' 'Oh yes! Thank you sir,' said Ali and picked up the fish.

He turned on his heel before Bert could speak and walked rapidly up the beach to disappear into his room, leaving Bert standing speechless by the boat. It was too late to do anything about it. Bert didn't have the heart to follow him and ask for his fish back!

As we left the Club on our way to Bert and Lilian's flat for a quickly revised menu of cold tuna fish, salad and chips, the appetizing odour of frying fish followed us down the road.

Bert was convinced that Ali had made a genuine mistake when he took the fish, and commented at length upon the simplicity and honesty of the unspoilt native boatman! He couldn't have been more mistaken! The following day all the waiters in the mess knew of the joke Ali had played upon Pashley sahib. John, my room boy, told me in great detail how Ali had played the joke on Bert. I didn't give him the satisfaction of knowing that Ali had taken my supper as well.

10

Sulaibikhat

Shortly after my arrival in Kuwait, I was moved from Shuwaikh to more senior quarters in Sulaibikhat Camp, the senior government residential camp some fifteen kilometres to the north of Shuwaikh. It was located outside of the city limits on the westerly coastline of Kuwait Bay.

The Housing Department offered me the opportunity to share a 'chummery', a single storey bungalow-type building with five bedrooms, a common sitting room, a dining room and a common bathroom. This accommodation was a considerable improvement over the block house accommodation provided in Shuwaikh Camp for the more junior government and contractors' employees.

A group of four or five bachelors occupied the accommodation, sharing the cost of servants and food. Each resident of a chummery took it in turn to serve a term as Mess President for a month at a time. His responsibilities were to organize the domestic staff, arrange the daily menus, purchase household stores and general groceries.

At the end of each month, the Mess President would prepare the individual mess bills for the residents.

These covered the cost of food, cleaning materials, servants' wages etc. Other members of the mess would take it in turns to act as Bar Member for similar periods. Their responsibilities were to maintain the stock of liquor by replacing the inventory of drinks consumed during the month by members of the mess and their guests. The worst aspect of these duties was the responsibility for preparing the monthly bar bills for settlement by the individual members of the mess.

A new member joining a chummery was required to advance five or six hundreed rupees, about thirty-eight pounds sterling at that time, towards the bar kitty. This sum enabled the Bar Member to provide an initial stock of liquor for the bar.

Whenever a resident or his guests had a drink, the resident would make out a chit stating the type and number of drinks they had consumed. At the end of the month the value of these chits would be totted up by the Bar Member, who would then issue a bill to each member of the mess for the liquor he and his guests had consumed.

Should a member of the mess leave, his initial payment would be reimbursed from the bar funds. Subsequently, his replacement would in turn purchase a similar share of the bar stock thus maintaining continuity.

Needless to say, this system rarely worked smoothly. There were continuous squabbles between the Bar Member and the other members of the mess. These disputes always revolved around whether or not a member had made out sufficient chits to cover his liquor consumption for the month.

Heavy drinkers usually forgot to make out a chit for every drink they had taken. Quite often, they underrated the number of drinks they had consumed during the month. Consequently, there would be a considerable discrepancy between the consumption as indicated by the chits received and the existing liquor stocks, as indicated by the monthly stock audit. Sometimes, when the discrepancies became a regular occurrence, the Bar Member took spot checks of drinks consumed and then personally added the unrecorded consumption onto the bill of the offending member!

When the offender saw the size of his bar bill at the end of the month, tempers would flare. Dark accusations involving the other members of the mess would be made. Sometimes members would not speak to each other for weeks on end and in extreme cases punches might be exchanged. Not a particularly pleasant situation!

In all innocence, and totally unaware of the problems that community living can generate, I accepted the offer and became the first resident of House No. 240 at Sulaibikhat, a pleasant house with blue painted steel framed windows and doors, and a double roof to provide some insulation from the heat of the desert sun, a great improvement on No. 8 Block at the Shuwaikh Camp.

The outer roof of the bungalow was constructed in galvanized steel sheeting, standing independently over the building on its own steel frame. This outer roof, extended over the house to form a shaded verandah, providing welcome shade from the intense heat and the glare from the sun. It also prevented the early morning and late evening sun shining directly into the rooms.

The inner roof or outer ceiling of the house was comprised of flat *chatti* matting sheets secured to creosoted lathes by reed or wire bindings. The *chatti* matting sheeting, composed of bundles of dried reeds harvested from the Iraqi marshes between the

Euphrates and the Tigris, was a popular construction material in the region. In some areas of Kuwait and of course in southern Iraq, whole villages of Barasti huts, hovels and rude shelters, were constructed in matting woven from the marsh reeds. In later years, the famous traveller, Frayer Stark, sailed down the Euphrates on a raft whose superstructure was fabricated from these marsh reeds.

With few exceptions, the majority of ceilings in the Kuwaiti houses of that period were made of this reed matting. The *chatti* matting ceilings, criss-crossed with a lattice work of black, creosoted lathes looked attractive to the western eye. However, they provided an ideal breeding ground for various insects, cockroaches, spiders and scorpions which from time to time would foray forth to plague the human residents of the accommodation. Particular care had to be taken during the hot, humid period between July and September. At this time it was not uncommon for scorpions to drop out of the matting onto the floor, creating a serious hazard for the unwary, barefooted resident.

When I arrived at the bungalow, three servants were already present. The butler, a smart looking Goanese of medium height with an outsize military moustache, answered to the name of Swami. He was the unchallenged head of the household staff. Swami organized the servants, waited on table and in general looked after the more important jobs of the house. As befitted the head of the household, he was always immaculately dressed in white trousers and shirt with a smart bow tie and matching cummerbund.

The cook, who answered to the name of Natty, short for Nathaniel, was a slow, simple man with an in-built delayed action response. When one spoke to him there was absolutely no reaction at all. Suddenly, a few moments later, he would reply. It was extremely difficult to hold a lucid conversation with him. His delayed responses relating to questions or comments prior to the current conversation were disconcerting to say the least. In order to continue a conversation with him, it was necessary to break one's train of thought, referring back three or four sentences in order to relate his answers to the conversation.

On one occasion, Ken, the mess officer of the month, sent Natty to buy the groceries for the week. Relying upon Natty's judgment as cook, Ken unwisely thought that it would not be necessary to provide him with a detailed shopping list. Needless to say, the mistake was never repeated! Natty spent the whole week's provision allowance on flour and sugar! For months, all our available cupboard space was full of packages of flour and sugar!

Although slow and perhaps not quite in touch with reality, to his credit, Natty was an excellent cook. He delighted in demonstrating his expertise at every possible opportunity. His speciality, like many of the Indian and Goanese cooks of the time, was in preparing dessert. They specialized in making ornate toffee baskets of caramelized sugar containing fruit salad and cream.

These were not ordinary baskets, but truly works of art. Natty would spend hours with a pan of hot caramelized sugar and water and a greased bottle as a mould, spinning and shaping strands of caramel toffee into ornate basket shapes. In addition to recognizable baskets, he would sculpt decorative cottages, schooners full sail, galleons, cars and even aeroplanes. Subsequently, they would appear on the dinner table brimming with fruit salad and cream. Natty would savour the compliment of our guests with the greatest pleasure, preening himself and promised to surpass this success at our next dinner party.

Abdullah was our sweeper. He carried out all the household tasks which were too menial for either the butler or the cook. He washed the floors, cleaned the toilets, polished the furniture and windows and cleaned the cars. He was also unofficial servant to the butler and the cook, cleaning and sweeping their quarters. The two senior servants were Goanese and Christian, Abdullah, on the other hand was Pakastani and a Muslim. Sadly, the two senior servants gave him a hard time, the Pakistani/Indian conflict was never far below the surface with them. In spite of this continuous pressure from his peers, Abdullah, a pleasant, cheerful boy of about sixteen or seventeen, was always willing to clean, fetch and carry at a moment's notice.

Shortly after I took up residence in the bungalow, the other members of the mess arrived. The first to come was Eric Jenkins, a shift engineer at the desalination plant. Eric was from South Wales. He was a keen photographer and a judo expert who had come to Kuwait to save a nest egg for his marriage the following year. Eric planned to return to Kuwait with his new wife after his first leave.

Bob Thwaites was the next to arrive. Bob, also a shift engineer, was previously employed by London Transport in their power station. Bob, like Eric and myself, had not previously been overseas, was married with a young family and hoped to be assigned married quarters within the year.

Jimmy Kinnell, shift engineer, and Ken Foxton, the Electrical Maintenance Engineer at the desalination plant arrived close on Bob's heels. Both Jimmy and Ken had been previously employed in Bahrain at the Caltex Refinery. They both spoke some Arabic, impressing us greatly with their apparent detailed knowledge of the Arabic world!

Some months later we were joined by Kingsley Jenkins, another Welshman and a friend, but not a relative, of Eric Jenkins. Kingsley was also a shift engineer and married. Unlike the rest of the group, he had no long-term plans for a career in Kuwait. Kingsley hoped to obtain a future place at a teachers' training college with a view to becoming a technical teacher later in his career.

Eric and I were the only two bachelors in the group. The other members were awaiting their turn to be either allocated married accommodation or to 'summer bride', by taking over someone's allocated house while the permanent residents were on leave. Once one had one's wife out in Kuwait, it was possible, by careful planning and some luck, to arrange a number of 'summer bride' situations in sequence, thus keeping one's wife in Kuwait throughout the qualifying period of one year, until the allocation of permanent married accommodation.

Considering the difference in ages and interests, and the fact that we worked and lived together, we managed to share the chummery without undue strife. Ken Foxton, Eric Jenkins, Bob Thwaites and myself were close friends throughout our stay in Kuwait. Jimmy Kinnell tended to be the odd man out. He already had friends in Kuwait City and preferred their company to that of his fellow members of the mess. Kingsley Jenkins, on the other hand, tended to be something of a loner and rarely mixed with us, preferring to spend his spare time reading in his room.

Our neighbours to the north and west were contractors' personnel, while over to the east lived Mustapha Sadiq, a colonel in the Kuwait Air Force.

Mustapha was the uncle of Queen Nariman of Egypt. She was a frequent visitor to his home and we often caught glimpses of King Farouk's mysterious and beautiful Queen.

Other close neighbours in the Sulaibikhat village were a group of Irishmen employed by the Ministry of Education. Two were particularly well-known characters. Brian was a gifted architect, young, good looking and musical, being quite a competent performer on the guitar. There was no doubt that he had kissed the Blarney Stone at some time in his career! He could charm a bird from a tree were he so minded. The single males in both Shuwaikh Camp and Sulaibikhat watched Brian's amorous successes amongst the limited number of single girls with a mixture of awe, jealousy and resentment.

Brian would set his cap at most of the eligible girls as a matter of course, but he had one ongoing interest in a particular girl who, at that time, would have little or nothing to do with him. Some years later, he finally won the day, and they were ultimately married. In the interim period, he comforted himself with the company of other single girls. To see Brian talking to one's girlfriend was like a sentence of doom. When this occurred the unlucky beau was immediately written off as the most recent has-been in the local romantic circles. Consequently, Brian was cordially hated by the males and adored by the girls.

One particular girl was enchanted by his good looks and winning chatter. Her father on the other hand, knew Brian only too well. He strictly forbade her to have anything to do with him. This of course only added a further incentive for the couple to meet secretly. One evening, when her father had presumably departed to play tombola at the Club, Brian arrived as previously arranged.

He parked at the rear of the house where the car would not be noticed. He knocked on the window and while waiting for his loved one to answer he glanced casually around. To his horror he saw her father's car still in the drive. Apparently, there had been a last minute change in plans and her father had not gone to tombola.

The front door lock clicked and Brian heard her father's voice demanding to know who was there? For a moment he froze, then panicked. He fled to his car, started the engine and without switching his lights on, drove down the hill away from the house. At the foot of the hill was a newly excavated drainage trench. Brian drove straight into it! The sound of the crash brought the nearest residents running from their houses to the scene of the accident. There in the bottom of the trench was Brian, sitting on top of his Morris Minor saloon idly strumming his guitar as though it was the most natural thing in the world for him to do.

In another amorous incident which did not proceed according to plan, he visited a girlfriend at her home while her parents were at a dinner party. So ardent was the love making that time was forgotten, and the parents returned before he could make his farewell. In a panic the young lady hid Brian in a wardrobe, hoping that he would be able to slip out when her parents went to bed.

Unfortunately, George, the father, had seen Brian's car standing at the rear of the house. In spite of his daughter's tearful protests, George proceeded to search the house, and finally unearthed Brian in the wardrobe in his daughter's bedroom. 'Hello George, nice to see you!' said Brian, full of self confidence and bravado. George never turned a hair. 'Come and have a drink,' he said, straight-faced, and led the way into the sitting room.

He poured the drinks and before sitting down opposite Brian, walked over to a sideboard, unlocked a drawer, and took out a large service revolver. He turned and sat opposite Brian, placing the revolver on the table between them. 'Brian,' he said pleasantly, 'if I ever catch you around my house again or hear that you have been talking to my daughter, I'll shoot you like a dog!'

George said afterwards that Brian looked at him for a moment, then, as he realized that George did not intend to shoot him, his confidence returned. Unperturbed, he finished his drink, drew himself up and said, 'If that's the way you feel George, then I'll say goodnight!' He stood up and walked to the door without a backward glance and strode out of the house with all the dignity that he could muster.

Shortly after this incident, George obviously not wishing to be placed in the position of making good his threat, took the precaution of sending his daughter back to England.

There was an Expatriate Club in Sulaibikhat. Not quite as large as the Shuwaikh Camp Club, but it was purpose-built with excellent facilities. It held two cinema evenings each week as well as a tombola evening. The residents of Shuwaikh Camp were regular visitors as it made a pleasant change to drive the few miles to Sulaibikhat to attend a cinema or play tombola. Wherever possible, the two Clubs arranged their various programmes in such a manner that their major events did not clash.

Alternate weeks, a Thursday evening dance was held in the open air on the terrace of the Expatriate Club. These dances were always popular, although evenings in July and August were usually extremely hot and humid. At such times the insects were always out in force. Colonies of bats dived and swooped on the fringes of the lights which attracted large numbers of winged and other insects.

Scorpions and beetles gathered in the sand beneath the boundary lamps. The large, desert-dwelling, predatory wolf spiders, such as jerimanders or camel spiders, were also attracted by the lights. They were fearsome looking beasts, in some instances as large as a spread hand, but relatively harmless. They earned their popular name of camel spider from the belief that they killed camels by biting them on the nose and were generally feared although their bite was little worse than a wasp sting.

On one particular occasion, Jeff Edgerton, a friend from work, came over to our table to say hello. Suddenly, one of the ladies screamed! Sitting on the shoulder of his white tuxedo was one of the largest camel spiders I have ever seen. Jeff casually turned his head and looked straight at the spider a few inches from his face. Obligingly, the spider reared up, waving its palps and no doubt gnashing its poisonous jaws!

Jeff let out a shriek which quite equalled that of the lady in both volume and pitch. Somehow, with unbelievable dexterity, he managed to divest himself of his tuxedo. In the wink of an eye he was standing two metres away looking back at his jacket while the coat was still in mid air, the spider was still sitting on its shoulder! The tuxedo fell to the floor and the spider scurried away under an adjacent table.

Then the panic started with ladies screaming and holding their skirts high and their feet off the floor. The braver of the men searched cautiously under the tables, ready for an instant fight should the spider appear. The whole evening was ruined. Conversation ceased. Everyone was too busy glancing uneasily around their feet and under the tables, in case the unwelcome guest should reappear and attempt to climb up their legs. Even the bravest periodically cast surreptitious glances under the table and around our feet.

One particular lady in the camp was inclined to imbibe a little too generously of the grape. Whenever Ethel went out to dinner or to a dance she was inclined to drink steadily throughout the evening, until suddenly, without any fuss or commotion, she would quietly fall asleep. The problem was at this stage it was almost impossible to awaken her. Nothing remained but for her husband to solicit the help of a couple of strong males to pack her into his car. When they arrived home, Ethel was far too heavy for him to lift her out of the car into the house, so it was his practice to leave her in the locked car to awaken in her own good time, while he went in to bed. In the early hours of the morning Ethel would awaken, leave the car, enter the house and go to bed as though nothing untoward had occurred.

On one particular dance evening, it became noticeable that ladies were leaving their tables and not returning. The ladies, by that time in varying stages of distress, were patiently queuing outside the ladies' toilet. Investigation showed that Ethel had gone to the only available toilet, locked the door and fallen fast asleep.

The annoyance of the distressed ladies, standing outside and hammering on the toilet door, the only response being Ethel's loud snoring, can only be imagined. Drastic measures had to be taken! For the remainder of the evening the gentlemen's toilet had to be designated as the ladies' lavatory on alternate half hours.

Shortly before the dance ended, Ethel appeared. She looked refreshed and quite sober. The irate ladies descended upon her like avenging angels, but Ethel was unperturbed. She refused to believe a word they were saying! As far as she was concerned she had only paid a routine visit to the toilet and left immediately. The other ladies, completely baffled by her indifference, retired in confusion.

11

The Storm

We had been resident in the chummery at Sulaibikhat for some ten weeks when the storm struck. Heavy storm clouds had started to gather during the previous days. But on this last day, they thickened rapidly until the sky was black, reducing the normally brilliant afternoon sunlight to a strangely ominous, murky haze. The sun appeared as a huge crimson disk, magnified to double its normal size by the haze.

The prevailing northerly breeze fell away into a foreboding dead calm. Not a breath of air stirred to alleviate the hot, humid atmosphere. Perspiration ran in rivers down our faces and dripped off the end of our noses. The overloaded air conditioning units could not cope with the excessive humidity. They either froze, due to the excessive moisture collecting upon their cooling coils, or clanked away fruitlessly, discharging hot, damp air into the room. It was obvious that a storm was brewing, but there was no indication whether it would be a thunderstorm, so characteristic of the time of year, or one of the major sandstorms that occurred from time to time.

The storm arrived during the early hours of the morning. I was awakened by a low, unfamiliar wailing noise. It seemed to pervade the whole house, like a giant kettle sighing on the hob. I climbed out of bed and looked through the window. The whole northern sky was alight with continuous flashes of sheet lightning. There was no accompanying sound of thunder, only the weird moaning wail, which seemed to originate from all directions at once. Strangely, not a breath of air stirred across the desert.

Glancing across the bay to the north, I caught sight of a movement in the almost continuous flashes of lightning. Intrigued, I waited for the next flash in the hope of identifying the moving object.

When it occurred, I was able to see the object clearly as it moved across the waters of the bay. Easily recognizable from the many books I had read and films I had seen, it filled me with a strange combination of excitement and fear. In the distance, perhaps ten or so miles away in the centre of the bay, but approaching rapidly across the water, was a jet black column stretching from the surface of the sea up to the cloud base. The almost continuous sheet lightning flashes produced a strobe light effect, resulting in the towering column appearing to be frozen in space. There was no mistake, the towering black column was the funnel of a tornado.

Noises in the passage outside my room indicated that the others were also awake. Quickly slipping on my clothes, I joined them in the sitting room. We stood by the French windows in the darkened room, gazing towards the north and watching the black column advancing slowly across the water towards us.

The low moaning grew in volume until it was louder than the whistle of an express train. The noise was doubly disturbing because of the deadly calm and lack of movement outside the house. We stood helplessly in the darkened sitting room, staring in silence out of the window.

No-one spoke; each of us concentrating upon his own thoughts, straining to see as much as possible with each flash of lightning. The black column approached rapidly, growing in size as it moved directly towards us.

Suddenly, there was a puff of dust in the sand outside the window. A strong gust of wind rattled the windows and doors. Then, with a loud crash of thunder and a roar of wind, the storm was upon us. The heavens opened and torrential rain fell in continuous sheets, like dark grey curtains in the lightning flashes.

The loud wailing noise, which had continued to gain in strength, reached a crescendo! The wailing gradually changed in timber until it was like the roar of escaping steam from a high pressure boiler. It roared and screamed around the house, shaking the building to its very foundations.

From above our heads came a rendering, tearing sound. It was as though the very house was being torn down around us. Through it all, we stood as though petrified. Physically, we were unable to move, so hypnotized were we by the power of the storm and the release of such enormous quantities of natural energy.

The torrential rain blowing against the glass of the window restricted our visibility to zero. It was no longer possible to see anything outside the house, although the lightning flashes and claps of thunder were almost continuous.

From time to time we would catch glimpses of debris flying in the wind. Sheets of corrugated iron, asbestos and rush matting, all obviously roofing materials, tore

132

past the window. Trash barrels, their contents flying along ahead of them, bowled along at express speed. Trees and shrubs so painstakingly planted around the houses by the residents, joined the host of articles madly rushing along before the wind.

Just as suddenly as it had arrived, the storm died. After the noise and confusion the calm was uncanny. The silence was broken at intervals by distant crashes of thunder. The howling wind was gone, just as though it had never been. Heavy rain still fell, but it now had a normality about it that was almost reassuring to our senses.

As usual with the British in times of excessive stress, our first action was to put the kettle on to make a pot of tea. In the fitful light of our torches, the power had failed, with steaming cups of strong tea to hand, we sat around the dining room table deciding what action we should take.

The storm had been so intense that it was obvious to us that severe damage must have been done throughout the City of Kuwait. Naturally, our first thoughts were for the safety and integrity of the distillation and power plant.

There was no power supply to the house and it was therefore logical to assume that the power station had been affected. We decided that our first priority was to go to the plant as quickly as possible to provide whatever assistance we could to alleviate any damage which had occurred. The major priority would be to reinstate water and power supplies to the city as quickly as possible.

Our plan of action formulated, we prepared to depart for the plant. I was first in the bathroom to shave and clean up prior to leaving. As I cleaned my teeth in the light of my torch, I casually glanced down at the floor.

To my intense horror and consternation, there between my bare feet on the tiles were two large, black scorpions.

I broke out in a cold sweat and leapt backwards. I had read somewhere that black scorpions were the most deadly of all. The various stories that I had heard concerning scorpion stings went through my head like a flash. At all times the stings were extremely painful, but if one were in poor health or allergic to the poison, the sting could be fatal. The venom of black scorpions was particularly virulent. All these thoughts passed through my mind more or less while I was in mid-air.

Like most rumours relating to to snakes and other poisonous creatures, there was only a smattering of truth in these tales. At the time I did not question a word. I picked up a conveniently placed lavatory brush and battered the scorpions as hard as I could until they disintegrated into unrecognizable pieces. No doubt the scorpions had either fallen from the rush matting of the ceiling, or had been driven out of the drains by the rising flood water.

Ken Foxton, who had much experience in such matters said that the *chatti* matting ceilings used to insulate the inner roof and ceiling in many buildings in Kuwait and the Arabian Gulf was an ideal habitat for scorpions, spiders, centipedes and other poisonous crawlers of the night.

These words were most encouraging to us all, particularly as the bedroom ceilings were all composed of similar material. Subsequently, long afterwards, whenever I went to bed, I would inspect the ceiling for any suspicious movement in the strands of the matting. I would then peer into the dark corners and crannies behind the bed and under the furniture. In the bathroom I would check behind the toilet bowl, the bath and hand basin. In the morning, before dressing, I would inspect my shoes, banging them vigorously on the floor before putting them on. Fortunately, all these precautions proved to be superfluous, I never had a positive find. Thank goodness!

We never encountered another scorpion in the house while we stayed there, but we regularly had visitations by the huge cockroaches popularly known as 'Bombay tigers', which are endemic in the Gulf region. They are filthy, unwholesome creatures living in the sewers and cesspits and gain access to the houses by means of the drains. Large ones can be between three and four inches in length. They usually appeared in the shower or toilet drains. It was not uncommon to be sitting enjoying a bath, only to find one of these unwelcome visitors sliding from the overflow to plop into the water beside one! Not pleasant, even for the hardier ones amongst us.

As the first light of dawn was breaking we left the bungalow to drive to the plant. The sight that greeted us outside the house was one of complete chaos. The roofs of houses and chummeries, including our own, had been torn off and blown away in the desert. A large piece of our roof had fallen onto my car! Fortunately, it had done little damage other than scratch the paintwork. Some other houses which had obviously not been in the direct path of the tornado had suffered only superficial damage. A number had their windows smashed by flying debris from the houses more directly in the path of the storm.

We started our engines and drove in a convoy towards the plant. Outside the Sulaibikhat Camp area it became apparent to us that the rest of Kuwait had only suffered a heavy rainstorm. There was no sign of any wind damage other than in the relatively narrow path that it had carved through the camp before departing across the desert. The roads were badly flooded and large expanses of water lay across the desert as far as the eye could see. In many sectors the road was completely submerged and its boundaries could not be seen. We drove along the crown of the road by feel alone, keeping clear of the ditches and the deep water at the side of the road, more by good luck than intent.

Upon reaching the plant, we were met by the Chief Engineer and the Plant Superintendent. They had been called out by the shift engineer when a number of areas had lost power supplies. This was as a result of rainwater causing short circuits whenever it entered switchgear and electrical junction boxes in the distribution system.

They were surprised to see us and to learn of the tornado, having assumed that this had only been a seasonal storm of above average severity. The windstorm had passed across the western section of Kuwait Bay, through Sulaibikhat Camp and disappeared into the desert. Fortunately, it had completely by-passed both the plant and the city.

We told them of our experiences and the damage that had occurred in Sulaibikhat. They found it hard to appreciate that such severe damage as we described could be isolated to such a small area as Sulaibikhat Camp, but our statements were soon corroborated by reports from the distribution engineers sent to repair the overhead power lines.

Jim Addison, the Chief Engineer, recalled that he had once experienced a similar situation in India where a tornado had passed through a village destroying all the houses on one side of the main street.

The houses on the opposite side were completely free from storm damage. He went on to warn us that storms and floods tended to drive snakes, scorpions, centipedes and camel spiders into the houses, seeking warmth and escape from the flood waters in the desert. He advised us never to walk outside at night in bare feet. Also, in case some uninvited guest had taken up residence over night, he impressed upon us the importance of always shaking one's shoes before putting them on in the morning.

For some considerable time after the storm and during subsequent rainy seasons, we noticed a dramatic increase in the number of incidents involving scorpions, camel spiders and snakes invading verandahs and porches; even gaining access to the living quarters through open doors and windows.

I told Jim Addison of my chance meeting with the scorpions in the bathroom and he said that I was extremely fortunate, commenting that the sting of a black scorpion was much worse than that of the larger light coloured one.

Snakes were particularly worrisome in Sulaibikhat. The majority of the desert snakes were russell vipers, a particularly poisonous species of snake. It was commonly found in the Kuwait desert where it normally lives in shallow burrows in the sand. During the winter season, in common with the scorpions and spiders, it seeks the warmth of the oil flow lines and gas flares near to the gathering centres. The oil workers are particularly careful when they approach the flow lines and gas flares during cold winter nights. The rain drives them to seek shelter under buildings and structures; hence their tendency to invade porches and balconies at such times.

The large wolf spider commonly found in the desert

is relatively harmless but tends to appear in the most disconcerting places. On one occasion, when we returned from the weekly dance at the Shuwaikh Club, one of our neighbours from the next chummery invited us in for coffee before retiring. We were all sitting in their lounge waiting for the coffee to be served, when Bill, one of the members of the mess called excitedly to us.

'Quickly! Come and see this,' he shouted from his bedroom. Dutifully, we joined him at the bedroom door. There, sitting in the centre of his room, apparently daring anyone to approach it, was one of the largest camel spiders that I had ever seen. It must have spanned at least eighteen centimetres from leg tip to leg tip and stood at least six centimetres off the floor. 'What should we do?' Bill asked. 'It might attack if we go near it, but we must remove it some way. I want to get to bed tonight!' he said.

'I'll move it,' said Tug Wilson, one of Bill's chummery mates. With no more ado, he took his shoes off and hurled one of them at the spider. The shoe missed the spider completely, but as Tug moved, it reared on its hind legs, waving its feelers or palps in the general direction of our group. Then suddenly, without any warning, it scuttled towards us, across the carpet, showing an amazing turn of speed.

We scattered in all directions. Tug, thinking that the beast was attacking him, dropped his second shoe which he had been about to throw, and bolted in a panic down the passage and out through the open front door, running barefoot into the desert night with the spider close on his heels. No doubt the spider was only trying to escape, but at that moment we could have sworn that it charged directly at Tug with malignant intent.

It was some considerable time later, in the early hours of the morning in fact, that Tug returned home. He had sought sanctuary in our chummery and would not return home until someone, equipped with a large pair of heavy boots and a lamp, had scouted out the route to ensure that the spider was not lying in wait for him.

Camel spiders are a species of wolf spiders. They hunt small birds, lizards, insects etc. by sight rather than by ensnaring their prey in webs as do most other spiders. Instinctively, our spider had focused in on Tug's movement. It had automatically moved towards Tug and then escaped into the desert in his wake through the front door. It is doubtful that it ever intended to attack him.

Some months later a further heavy storm struck Kuwait. The storm was preceded by a shower of huge hailstones. The ice particles were as large as golf balls. Many sheep and goats were killed in the desert where they could not find adequate shelter from the falling ice. In Kuwait City many vehicles were damaged by the large hailstones, bodywork was dented and windscreens were shattered. After the hailstorm came three days of torrential rain which in itself exceeded Kuwait's average annual rainfall.

In those early days, Kuwait, like most Gulf towns of the period, lacked an effective drainage system. Even the smallest rainfall resulted in flooded roads and alleyways. The narrow, unsurfaced streets would become impassable quagmires as the iron hard *gatch*, the local calcium sulphate bearing clay, absorbed the rain water, forming a soft, cream textured mud. Cars and trucks would become bogged down, blocking streets while the ankle deep mud made walking difficult and unpleasant.

Sunbaked *gatch* had been used to build the older Kuwaiti houses. Excessive exposure to the heavy rain resulted in these older buildings collapsing as the *gatch* softened, often with tragic consequences.

A further hazard involved the electrical systems. The locals had little or no regard for the science and theory of electricity. If they required a power connection or another lamp, they would simply make a connection using any wire that was available. If the system was overloaded and the fuses blew, they would put in larger fuses. In many instances they simply used pieces of wire, or even nails. Consequently, circuit protection was virtually non-existent in many houses. When a short circuit did occur, it usually resulted in electro-cution or a major fire. Certain areas of the city were so prone to such accidents that the Ministry automatically cut off the local power supply whenever it rained. Unpopular as this was, the procedure certainly saved many lives.

The outlying roads from the city were also seriously affected by the rains. The majority of these roads were generally raised on an embankment above the general level of the desert. Low lying areas flooded within hours of the rain starting and at such times there was no way of knowing how deep the water was, or where the edges of the roads were under the muddy water. Approaching one of these submerged sections of road was like playing Russian Roulette! If one was lucky enough to remain on the road, the water was only a few inches deep. Stray off the edge of the road and the water could be three or four feet deep.

One evening, driving home from the cinema, our headlights picked out a group of familiar figures standing beside the road in their undershorts, evening shirts and bow ties! A group of consulting engineers had been out to a dinner party at Sulaibikhat Camp. On their way home, a little the worse for wear after a surfeit of good food and wine, they had run into a flooded section of the road. Driving too fast, water had splashed onto the distributor and the engine had stalled. So as not to wet their clothes, they had taken off their trousers, shoes and socks, while they pushed the car out of the water onto a drier section of the road. At least that was their plan.

Unfortunately, they had pushed the car, containing their clothes, off the edge of the road into water some four feet deep. When we arrived on the scene only the roof of their car was showing above the water. They stood helpless and shivering in the cold night air, their trousers and jackets submerged in the car.

After making the most of their embarrassment by pulling their legs unmercifully, much to the disgust and chagrin of the unfortunate flood victims, we gave them a lift home. We could do nothing for their vehicle or their clothing. The following day a heavy tow truck was sent out to pull their car from the mud, back onto the road.

After the storm, things gradually returned to normal. The flood waters drained away and the insects and snakes returned to the desert. Summer was over at long last, and the searing temperatures of August and September disappeared to be replaced by warm, sunny days and cold, clear nights. The expatriate community were once again able to participate with comfort in various indoor activities. It was the amateur dramatic and operatic season. The dramatic and operatic societies occupied the leisure time of a majority of the expatriate community. They participated in various productions with a mixed degree of success.

12

The Amateurs

In Kuwait at that time, there were many highly talented
people ready to give time and effort to entertain the
community. There were also many quite untalented
people who delighted in the opportunity to take part in
a stage production. Whatever their reason or their
degree of talent, the members of the societies did a
worthwhile job, entertaining the expatriate community.

One particular lady had at one time been a
professional actress. Sadly, the years had taken their
toll. Time had dulled both her memory and hearing,
making her involvement on the local stage more of a
liability than an asset to the remainder of the cast. She
no longer had the ability or concentration necessary to
carry her through the full length of a play.

Usually she made an excellent start, but as the play
progressed her memory would begin to betray her. She
would miss lines, sometimes even ad-lib with lines
from other plays, much to the confusion and
consternation of the other actors. Over the months and
years, she and her husband were long-serving
expatriates on permanent posting in Kuwait, the
condition gradually deteriorated and each play

became progressively worse.

Unfortunately for the sanity and good temper of the producers and directors, her desire to perform on stage seemed to increase as her ability decreased. She was always ready to audition for parts, being the first to arrive and the last to leave casting meetings.

At that particular time, the Kuwait Dramatic Society were producing *The Mousetrap* for the first time in Kuwait. The lady in question had auditioned and been given one of the leading parts in the production. The producer and director, recent arrivals in Kuwait, were obviously impressed by her past experience, while her stage presence at the audition made them believe that they had discovered a local star! They were soon to discover the error of their decision to use her in a major role.

Each evening, before going on stage she would partake of a large brandy. 'To relax the vocal chords, dear!' she would explain to all and sundry. She would then totter onto the stage where, without fail, she would forget major proportions of her lines. Sometimes she would dry up completely and stand helpless and mute in centre stage.

Being slightly deaf, she could not hear the prompt. This resulted in long pregnant pauses, during which the other members of the cast either tried desperately to provide her with a prompt or ignoring her completely, gloss over the missing dialogue as best they could. The situation was exacerbated by the fact that at each performance she forgot her lines in a different part of the script. Long before the final performance, the director was in a complete state of nerves. It was strongly rumoured that he had taken to heavy drinking before each performance!

In desperation they finally relocated the prompt in

the chimney breast at the centre of the set. The producer arranged for the actress to stand by the fireplace; delivering all her lines from this point without moving around the room as previously. Foolishly, he assumed that this would solve the problem.

The following morning, after a particularly large brandy, she tottered onto the stage to take up her assigned position by the fireplace. As expected, she soon forgot her lines. The prompt acted immediately, whispering the lines to her from his seat in the chimney breast, some two or three feet from her.

Nothing happened! She merely stood there in the centre of the stage gazing desperately around. After a number of attempts to give her the correct line, each delivered in a louder voice than before, the prompt intoned the line in a voice which could be heard at the back of the hall. She poked her head up the chimney. 'I'm sorry, dear,' she said in a loud stage whisper that also echoed around the hall, 'you will have to speak louder.' The audience broke into a roar of uncontrolled laughter. Word soon circulated and people flocked to see the comedy version of *The Mousetrap* which became one of the major successes of the Kuwait stage.

We were never short of trauma at the theatre! The audience always took these problems and mistakes in good part. Although they laughed and joked about it, there was never unkind criticism. Everyone appreciated the efforts of the few to entertain the many. There were many talented people amongst the expatriate community who were always prepared to give freely of their time and skills to entertain the less gifted of us.

Everyone tried to support the efforts of the amateur groups. The members of our chummery were no exception. Our services were in demand for various support activities both on and behind the stage. As a chemist my services were required for special effects: mainly to provide flashes, explosions and smoke. Ken Foxton being an electrical engineer, was regularly on demand to provide wiring and new lighting systems and Eric Jenkins was always ready to take part in the various plays.

On one particular afternoon, the Back Stage Committee comprising mainly ladies, arranged to visit us at the chummery. They wished to discuss arrangements for the special effects and lighting for a new production of *Cinderella* that was about to go into rehearsal.

The ladies arrived rather earlier than expected, shortly after Ken and I had arisen from our afternoon siesta.

The meeting was held in the lounge where we had arranged for tea and biscuits to be served by the houseboy. The lounge area was separated from the dining room by a draw curtain, which we closed to allow the houseboy to lay the table for the evening meal without disturbing the meeting.

During a lull in the conversation, I heard a door in the corridor from the bedrooms open and close, followed by the pad of bare feet. The footsteps seemed to enter the kitchen. A refrigerator door banged. Then, glasses clinked in the dining room on the other side of the curtain where the bar was located. Obviously, one of our fellow residents had arisen from his siesta and wanted a drink after his afternoon doze.

There was a brief silence, then the curtains rustled. We paused, all expecting to see one of our friends, glass in hand, appear through the curtain. The curtains rustled again and then slowly parted. A large, white pair of buttocks appeared between the drapes.

Everyone, including the ladies, gazed uncomprehendingly at the sight! Then the offending item broke wind loudly. A voice, which the members of the mess instantly recognized, said, 'Share that between you!' The buttocks slowly withdrew, the curtains fell back into place and we heard the footsteps padding back into the passage. Then a bedroom door opened and closed leaving us sitting in silence, looking at each other.

We sat in shocked silence for at least a couple of minutes, completely overcome by the unexpected nature of the incident. The situation was made worse by an almost uncontrollable desire to laugh. To their credit, the ladies never turned a hair! After what seemed to be an age, just as though nothing had happened, one of the ladies picked up the conversation where we had left off some minutes before.

The other ladies quickly followed her example. We, of course, were totally embarrassed. Somehow Ken and I controlled the urge to burst into wild laughter. With great difficulty, we followed the ladies' example not daring to catch each other's eye in case we lost control. Needless to say, the meeting didn't last too long after this! The ladies concerned never once mentioned the incident to us at that time or later.

As soon as the ladies left, we raced up the corridor to the room of our recent visitor. At first he would not believe that there had been ladies present throughout his performance. When we finally convinced him of the fact, he was quite horrified and accused us of keeping quiet in order to embarrass him!

He was particularly worried in case the ladies had recognized him. When he received our assurance that this was most unlikely, he swore us to secrecy, demanding that we would not reveal his name under any circumstances.

It was a major topic of conversation at the Dramatic Society for long afterwards. Many attempts were made to worm the identity of the culprit from us, but to no avail. Although the ladies themselves never mentioned it directly, their various husbands took great delight in repeating the story, suitably embellished, of course, to add spice and colour to the tale. Fortunately, Ken Foxton and myself had a cast iron alibi provided by the ladies themselves. The other members of the chummery were the object of the gravest suspicion and for long afterwards were subjected to a variety of trick questions in attempts to worm out the name of the culprit.

13

Married Life

While on one of my annual leaves, I met my future wife, Edith Kay. It was a chance meeting at the la Casablanca, a small coffee shop in Bolton town centre, where she worked at weekends. Edith was an artist by profession in a company associated with one of the leading gent's outfitters in Lancashire.

The la Casablanca Coffee Bar was at that time the 'in place' where the youth of the town gathered to see and be seen. Some days previously, I had managed to obtain tickets for the film *South Pacific* being shown in Todao. The film was currently being shown in Manchester and was such an outstanding success that every performance was fully booked. The girl that I had intended to take with me was unable to go and it seemed a shame to waste a ticket.

When Edith served the coffee that I had ordered, I took a chance and invited her to accompany me to see the film. To my surprise she accepted immediately. I later learnt that she was deeply involved in amateur dramatics and was desperately hoping to see the film.

South Pacific was superb in every respect. We enjoyed it so much that we decided to see it again. In all we saw it twelve times in a two year period. One thing led to another and we began to date regularly, whenever I returned home to the UK. Gradually, things became more serious between us and we considered getting engaged. Firstly though, we had to find out if she would like to live abroad away from her friends and the amenities of the UK.

In 1960, I invited Edith to come out to Kuwait for a holiday and she accepted. My dearest friends in Kuwait, the Woolley family in Ahmedi, kindly offered to accommodate and chaperon her throughout her stay. She would live with them in Ahmedi, the Kuwait Oil Company's residential town and I would drive the twenty-six miles from Shuwaikh to the Woolley's house each afternoon to see her.

As quickly as possible, I arranged the necessary visa and sent her the return air ticket for the journey. At long last, on the prearranged day in June, the Woolleys and Sonnie and Jim Worthington together with most of my friends from the Kuwait City assembled with me at the airport in readiness to meet her.

The turbo-prop Bristol Britannia *The Whispering Giant,* from London, arrived on schedule. The Kuwait summer weather did not disappoint us and the 125 degrees Fahrenheit shade temperature must have struck her like a physical blow as she descended the steps from the aircraft. Fortunately, she quickly cleared the customs and passport formalities and we were able to return to the Woolley's air conditioned home without delay.

The Woolleys in their generosity made her extremely welcome and immediately accepted her into the heart of their family. Cath Woolley and Sonnie Worthington took Edith everywhere with them; introducing her to all their friends in the oil company. Pat and Ian, Harry and

Cath Woolley's children, also did their part. They became her firm friends and invited her to join in all their activities while I was at work down in Kuwait.

Some days after Edith's arrival, I received a call from Abdul Latif, the Chief of Kuwait Security, requesting that I go to see him. I went immediately. To receive a call from so important an official was unusual, but as I knew him well I did not put too much emphasis on the summons.

The following morning, as requested, I arrived at the Security Building and was shown immediately into Abdul Latif's office. We shook hands and he waved me to a seat. Unusually, after being served with the usual mint tea, he omitted the usual small talk and pleasantries and got down to business straight away. Normally, it was local custom to indulge in small talk and pleasantries for some time before tackling the main subject of a meeting. Not this time!

'Tom, I am very upset and disturbed that you should embarrass me in this way,' he said abruptly. 'I gave you a visa for your friend, never thinking that you would bring someone of this type to Kuwait!'

He must have noted my puzzled expression, because he continued. 'You know our attitude to such things. Why did you bring a striptease dancer into Kuwait? You should never have done so, particularly on a visa that I gave you!'

'There must be some mistake,' I told him. 'Edith's a designer. What on earth made you think that she is a striptease dancer?'

'It says so in her passport,' he told me, pointing to the document lying on his desk. 'Look!' he opened the passport and pointed to the section referring to occupation. 'See, it clearly states "Display Artist"! That's clear enough, isn't it?'

150

I must admit it was extremely difficult to keep a straight face, but I managed to do so. Once he realized his mistake, he would have assumed that I was laughing at him, embarrassing him even further.

It took considerable discussion and explanation to persuade him that 'Display Artist', at least in this case, meant a designer of displays and sets for commercial exhibitions. In actual fact I am sure he grasped the true import of the meaning immediately I pointed it out to him, but in order to save face, he was prepared to argue and procrastinate for a considerable time before he finally decided that he should accept the argument.

For many years afterwards, whenever I met Abdul Latif, he would refer to my striptease dancer, taking great delight in telling everyone that I had imported a 'Stripper' to Kuwait!

As it was Edith's twenty-first birthday on July 5th, the Woolleys kindly offered to host a party at their home to celibrate the event. The night before the party, we were all sat down at dinner, when Harry Woolley said, 'You know, last night I had a strange dream! I dreamt that Pat was getting married. The church was full of oil pipelines, but the bride was nowhere to be seen!'

I felt quite uncomfortable. I was not particularly superstitious, but I recalled my mother and my grandmother, both of whom believed in such things, saying to dream of a wedding meant a death. Neither Harry nor Cath had any idea of this at all. Apparently, Edith had also heard of this interpretation to the dream, because she cautioned me to be careful when I drove home that evening. Harry's remarks about his dream brought a twinge of unease, but when I arose the following morning the incident was forgotten.

The party was a great success. After work, armed with my present, I drove up the road to Ahmedi and the

Woolley's house. We had a lovely time, everyone enjoyed themselves. The party concluded around 1.00 a.m., with everyone saying good night and making their way home.

The following morning was Friday and the Kuwaiti weekend. After breakfast, I drove back to Ahmedi and was met at the door by Harry Woolley who was extremely upset. It seemed that his daughter's boyfriend of the time, an architect working with the oil company, had driven home from the party in his MG, taken a corner too fast and somsersaulted the car.

The company medical examiners found that he had advanced tuberculosis and a weak heart. The shock of turning the car over had brought on a heart attack. When they found him, he was dead behind the wheel. Apparently, earlier he had had a puncture and not having a spare wheel had borrowed a wheel and tyre from a friend. The odd wheel had obviously contributed to the accident.

Poor Pat was traumatized. It was a terrible time for her and the Woolley family as a whole. Because he was diagnosed to have suffered from tuberculosis prior to his death, Pat, the whole family and anyone who had been in contact with him, had to be subjected to a series of tests. Fortunately, all proved to be clear of any infection.

It took a long time for Pat to get over the tragedy. Time cures everything, and some years later she met and married a petroleum engineer. Returning to England, they raised a delightful family and lived happily ever after.

Harry's dream of the previous evening and the accident may only be a coincidence, but it certainly made one wonder whether there is more to the interpretation of dreams than we sceptics think!

Shortly after this tragic accident, Edith and I became engaged. Then Edith went home to arrange our wedding for the following January. We were married at the Parish Church in Bolton.

For our honeymoon we flew to Zurich, Switzerland by De Havilland *Comet* and then travelled by train to Wengen, in the Swiss Oberland. I had reserved a double room with bath at the Alpenrue Hotel in Wengen, a picturesque alpine village, set on the side of the Manlichen, facing Lauterbrunnen across the valley, famous for the Trumelbach Falls where Sherlock Holmes and Moriarty perished.

Our room at the hotel had glorious views of the Jungfrau, Monch and Eiger mountains. There were no cars or roads in the village, only footpaths. People either walked or rode toboggans shouting 'Atchung! Atchung!' as they tore down the snow-covered paths. On my first day in Wengen, I experienced an encounter with one such party. Edith and I were walking down to the village from the hotel, when suddenly there was a wild cry of 'Atchung!' from behind me. There was a sudden blow at the back of my legs and my feet lost their precarious purchase on the impacted snow of the path. My legs shot up in the air and I fell backwards onto a soft resilient bundle comprising two ladies and a small child.

Arms and legs waving wildly, we tore down the hill, completely out of control. Fortunately, the path was not straight. At the first bend, before we could pick up too much speed, we shot off the path into a snow drift. A snow bank broke our speed bringing us to a sudden stop and we arose from the soft snow, shaken, but unhurt.

It was some time before we found out why the other guests weren't at all well disposed towards us.

Apparently, when I had reserved a double room with a bath, to oblige us the management had assigned the main bathroom in the hotel to our room. The other guests were then forced to go to the upper floor of the hotel where another bathroom was located. Not too pleasant in the dead of night, when the outside temperature was forty degrees below zero.

After a most memorable honeymoon we returned to Kuwait. While we had been away the Woolleys and other friends had prepared our house for our return. Within a few days we were settled in like an old married couple.

Life as a married couple was far different to that of a single person. In the eyes of the Arab, marriage provided an umbrella of respectability. Unless one was a family friend of long standing, it was most unlikely that a single man would ever be invited to meet the family of a local Arab. If a bachelor was privileged to be invited to the home of a local Arab, he would sit in the *majlis,* a large conference or meeting room, with the male members of the family and their male friends. He would never meet or see the females of the family.

With a wife things changed drastically. As man and wife, we were regularly invited to Arab homes and made many lasting family friendships.

Within a short while, Edith settled comfortably into life in Kuwait. Her days were always full of things to do. She taught ballet to both British and local children, became involved in voluntary services for the British Ladies Society, worked in the library associated with the British School and completely filled her day. When we moved to Saudi Arabia she became actively involved in running the local Girl Guides and along with Lady Morris, the then Ambassador's wife, started a Sunday School in the Embassy compound. An unheard of thing in Saudi Arabia!

During our stay in Kuwait we had two children – a son, Tom and a daughter, Elizabeth. Like Edith and I, they enjoyed every moment of their stay in the Middle East and still look back with the greatest affection for the people, the places and the times spent there.

14

John Paul Getty

J. Paul Getty was a slim, elderly, self-made American who never seemed to smile. Reputedly, he had four main interests in his life. They were oil, money, beautiful women and weight training. He once said it was his unsatisfied ambition to be a champion weightlifter. Up to a short time before his death and in spite of his extremely demanding business routine, he always found time for a daily weight training workout. Each year, he made a point of attending the annual Mr Universe contest in London, where he was an enthusiastic spectator.

It was here that I first met Paul Getty. I was also a keen weight trainer, and being one of the early members of the National Amateur Body Builders' Association, I was usually invited to their various functions.

One year, the National Amateur Body Builders' Association invited Mickey Hargitay to enter the Mr Universe contest. He accepted and brought his wife, Jayne Mansfield, the Hollywood film star, with him. After the show, which Mickey won, the couple were invited to attend the annual Mr Universe dinner to be held at the Royal Hotel in Woburn Place, London. Paul

Getty, amongst other celebrities, was also invited.

After a convivial dinner and many speeches, the evening drew to a close. The various guests went their separate ways. The Hargitays drove off in their rented Rolls Royce, I collected my car that I had parked outside the hotel. It was a pillar box red Lincoln Continental, my pride and joy for many years. I had recently driven the car back to England from Kuwait and thoroughly enjoyed the stir it made as I drove through the UK streets.

Paul Getty stood on the pavement in the rain waiting for a taxi. It was rumoured that he objected to paying his driver overtime and not wishing to drive himself,he was forced to use public transport when out after normal office hours.

At the time, I thought how strange that the richest man in the world, as Getty was at the time, would not have his own car and driver waiting for him. Later, after getting to know both Getty and a number of other extremely wealthy men quite well, I understood his attitude a little better.

It would seem that once a certain amount of wealth has been acquired, it ceases to have a fiscal meaning. Like Monopoly money, additional assets become simply a monitor of either success or failure in the Wealth Game, which tycoons play with such great enthusiasm.

People like Paul Getty, Suliman Olayan and other extremely wealthy individuals, appear to have little interest in spending money. Their absorbing interests are acquisition and winning. Figuratively speaking, their object in life appears to be having a greater amount of counters, or money, at the end of the day than they had at the beginning. As long as their day-to-day needs are met, and in many cases these are

157

surprisingly simple, they have little or no interest in spending for spending's sake.

Suliman Olayan, a Saudi Arabian business tycoon, is a shining example of this philosophy. With unbelievable wealth at the age of sixty-five, Suliman works sixteen hours a day, week in, week out. His personal needs are spartan to the extreme. When I knew him, he drove an old Mercedes and lived in rented accommodation. He was not a mean man, but had little regard to the panoplies of wealth.

At the time in question, John Paul Getty was the owner of the Tidewater Oil Company, The Pacific Western Oil Company and the Getty Oil Company. In 1949 he paid US$10,500,000 for a half share in the neutral zone concessions lying between Kuwait and Saudi Arabia.

He was forced to spend a further US$30,000,000 before his company found oil in commercial quantities. When oil was finally found, it was present in such vast amounts that within a short time he became a billionaire and subsequently the world's richest man.

Getty was an unusual person in many ways. Extremely successful in business, he seemed to be totally devoid of any success in his personal and emotional life. After his fifth marriage ended in failure, he rationalized his relationships with women to less formal arrangements and concentrated with greater intensity upon increasing his wealth and holdings in the oil business that he knew so well.

John Paul Getty had a fear of flying. Unlike most people who dislike travelling in aeroplanes and overcome their fear of flying out of necessity, Getty would not compromise his dislike of air travel. Consequently, he reduced his overseas travel to a minimum and then only travelled by ship and road. When he visited his oil holdings in Kuwait and the neutral zone, he would sail to Beirut and then drive by car along the trans-Arabian pipeline to the neutral zone, about three days' driving. Otherwise, he would send his son, George, to represent him.

In the course of one of George Getty's visits, an employee had an accident on the road into Kuwait City. Unfortunately, he killed a Kuwaiti pedestrian while driving to the bank in Kuwait City to collect the monthly payroll. By law he should not have left the scene of the accident. Because he had been drinking and feared that he would be arrested when the police arrived, he left without giving his name and employer to any of the witnesses which were gathering there. He then drove with all speed back to the Getty installation at Mina Saoud.

Upon his return, he reported the accident to the General Manager who in turn alerted George Getty. He did not tell them that he had been drinking prior to the accident, or that he had left the scene without giving his name.

In an effort to help his employee and save him from what might be a mandatory prison sentence, George arranged for the man to take immediate overseas leave. A seat on a plane leaving later that day was booked by phone, and within an hour the employee was on his way to the airport, where he took the flight leaving for Europe.

Some three or four hours later, the Kuwaiti police arrived at Mina Saoud. An alert bystander had taken the number of the truck and reported it. When they arrived in Mina Saoud, the police found their quarry had flown. Naturally, they took a somewhat jaundiced view of the whole episode. George was summoned to attend an interview at the police headquarters in Kuwait, where a full enquiry into the matter was to be held.

When he refused to attend the hearing, he was arrested and taken into custody in place of the man he had released. Although his name and position soon ensured his release, the experience soured his attitude to Kuwait and the Arab world in general. Immediately he was released from custody, he returned to the United States and never returned to Kuwait again.

As a result, Paul Getty decided to take charge himself. He drove out to Kuwait from Europe by car with his close friend of the time, Miss Penelope Kitson. The journey was extremely long and tiring and must have done little to improve Mr Getty's opinion of the Middle East and Saudi Arabia in particular.

In those days, an oiled sand and dirt road ran alongside the trans-Arabian pipeline across great tracts of desert. The only available accommodation for rest and refreshment throughout the journey was to be found at the various pumping stations, strategically located along the pipeline route. Although the accommodation was crude, the staff at the pumping stations made every visitor welcome. Their generous hospitality reflected their delight to see a new face and hear news from the outside world. Nevertheless, in spite of this surfeit of hospitality the trip was extremely arduous and taxing even for a young person and Paul Getty was certainly not a young man.

Even when Paul Getty arrived in the neutral zone, his ordeal was not over. The car broke down on the road between the trans-Arabian pipeline and the Getty Oil Camp at Mina Saoud, stranding them in the desert. Fortunately, they were rescued before any serious problems could arise, but Paul Getty's temper was not improved by the incident.

Upon arrival at Mina Saoud they ate, showered and slept. The following day was spent sleeping and lazing on the beach, recovering from the ordeal of the marathon car drive. Paul Getty then applied himself totally to reorganizing the operations of his company. Within a year of his visit, his drilling crews struck oil at the rate of 16,000,000 barrels per year. But in the oil business, success only breeds further problems.

Unfortunately, the crude oil from the Wafra field contained considerable quantities of hydrogen sulphide gas and salt. A combination which made the oil extremely corrosive to metal and difficult to handle. Sea-going tankers, including his own ships, would not accept the unprocessed crude oil from his oilfield. This caused Paul Getty considerable embarrassment, as well as no little loss of revenue.

In order to ensure that the crude oil would be accepted as cargo, it became necessary to wash the oil free of salt before it was loaded into the ships.

As referenced earlier, the Getty oil operations were located at Wafra in the waterless desert of the neutral zone, some thirty-six miles from the coast, while the shipping point was at Mina Saoud, on the coast. The water required to wash the oil had to be shipped in gigantic road tankers from Kuwait City, across some ninety miles of rough desert tracks. Logistically, this mammoth operation was expensive and fraught with difficulties.

One day, Captain Holden, a retired British Naval Officer and the Getty Oil Company Manager of the time, walked into my office. He was a polished and charming gentleman, chubby, stoop shouldered and with extremely poor eyesight. It was difficult to imagine how he could ever hope to control such an operation as

161

the Getty Oil Company and its crew of rough, tough, Texan drillers, roughnecks and roustabouts. A John Wayne type would have seemed to be more appropriate for the post!

Always considerate and polite in his approach to people, it was only when one had the chance to see the steel that lay below the gentle veneer, that it became easy to understand why Paul Getty had entrusted his whole Arabian operation to this rather frail, short-sighted, retired Naval Captain. He was well-liked and highly respected by all the Getty staff at both Mina Saoud and Wafra.

Captain Holden told me that he was faced with a major problem in obtaining a sufficient quantity of water at Wafra to meet the company's needs. Paul Getty had suggested that he contact me with a view to finding a solution to the problem.

I was intrigued by the potential of the project and agreed to help. Before Captain Holden left to return to the neutral zone, we arranged that I would travel to Mina Saoud that coming weekend to review the facilities available and commence my evaluation of the problem.

The following Friday, as arranged, I started out for the neutral zone and the Getty Camp at Mina Saoud. Prior to leaving, like any sensible citizen, I informed the various authorities of my intended destination, the time that I expected to arrive and a tentative time for my return to Kuwait City.

The Getty Oil Company's operational headquarters was at Mina Saoud some eighty miles south of Kuwait City. There was a metalled road for some fifty per cent of the journey. The remainder of the trip was over desert tracks with surfaces ranging from hard, ribbed, *gatch* to soft, sandy stretches, where a careless driver could easily become bogged down.

162

The road to Mina Saoud was asphalted only as far as Ahmedi, the Kuwait Oil Company township. Beyond Ahmedi, the well metalled road was reduced to a narrow sandy track that followed the coast, within sight of the sea. Sections of the track ran across areas of *subqua* or salt marshes. In the dry period, these areas were iron hard and a pleasure to drive over, but during the rainy period they became deep quagmires of saline mud. At such times, cars, whose drivers were foolish enough to attempt to cross them, would become trapped, sinking deep into the soft liquid mud, sometimes up to their roof tops. Fortunately, the drivers were usually able to escape with their lives.

The *gatch*, like the *subqua*, in the presence of moisture turned the material into a soft plastic mud. As one travelled further south, the surface of the desert changed from gravel to sand. Here, the track crossed many areas of soft sand.

One had to drive over these areas at high speed. Should the momentum be lost for any reason, the vehicle would founder in the soft sand, the wheels would sink and the vehicle would become bogged down, sometimes even to the level of the chassis. It would have to be dug out by hand, or towed out, if one was fortunate enough to locate a truck with large enough wheels to negotiate the soft sand with impunity.

Unfortunately, as I approached one of these areas of soft sand, another car appeared in the distance. It was speeding along from the opposite direction and like myself, the driver was so intent upon the road that he did not see me approaching until it was almost too late. At the last minute, to avoid running headlong into him, I had to swerve violently off the narrow track. Consequently, I ran headlong into the deep sand lying at the side of the rough road. In spite of my efforts to use the car's momentum to return to the relatively hard surface of the track, the car settled down in the soft sand up to the chassis level.

I climbed out to inspect the damage and watched the other car career off unheedingly in a cloud of dust. I turned my attention back to my own vehicle. There was just no way that I would be able to dig it out on my own. I was stuck there in the middle of the desert with no help in sight.

The reflected heat from the white sand was so intense that the perspiration oozing from my pores dried immediately. My skin was left dry and rough to the touch. My face was white with a rime of dried salt. The heat haze danced across the desert sand making the horizon blurred and indistinct.

'Dust Devils' spun and played across its surface like miniature whirlwinds. Lawrence of Arabia once called the desert 'The sun's anvil'. He wasn't wrong. The sun beat down striking me with the intensity of a physical blow. The reflected heat supplemented the sun's heat until the very air seemed to vibrate.

Feeling completely helpless, I stood contemplating my fate, hoping and praying that someone would come along before I developed heat exhaustion and collapsed from dehydration. The car was so badly bogged down in the soft sand that there was no hope of digging it out or pulling it free with anything less than a large truck. My chances were indeed slim. In the height of the summer, and at the weekend, people rarely travelled these desert tracks. The majority of people would be either lazing on the beach, or sitting peacefully at home in the comfort of their air conditioning. It might be the following day before anyone came this way!

I was just rationalizing my problems, when a voice behind me said, 'Hi, Tom! You sure seem to have a problem.' I spun round, startled. A welcome figure stood before me, it was Chuck Williams, the gigantic drilling boss of the Getty Oil Company. A few yards away was Chuck's transport, a huge four-wheel drive Kenworth truck, the engine idling sweetly. I had been so preoccupied with my problems that I had not heard Chuck drive up.

I explained what had happened and told Chuck that I was on my way to see Captain Holden at Mina Saoud. 'No problem,' said Chuck, 'I have a tow line in the cab. I'll pull you out in no time flat!'

True to his word, Chuck had a tow cable fixed to my car within minutes. Initially he placed it around the front bumper, fender Chuck called it, but it proved to be inadequate for the job! When Chuck reversed the Kenworth truck the tow cable tightened, but the car did not move. Instead, with a squeal of torn metal, the front bumper of my car broke free and bumped across the desert in the wake of the truck.

After placing the dislodged bumper in the boot of my car, we tried again. This time Chuck produced a shovel from the cab of the Kenworth and set to work clearing the sand from beneath the car, until he could reach underneath to secure the tow cable around the chassis. I had a terrible thought that my front axle might join the bumper in the boot. Fortunately, my fears were unfounded. With considerable creaking and juddering the car slowly emerged from the soft sand.

Once the car was back on the harder surface of the track I thanked Chuck profusely, being sure that he had saved my life. Chuck treated it as a routine matter that was hardly worth mentioning. My gratitude and thanks expressed, we disengaged the cable and I continued my journey to the Getty Camp at Wafra, following closely in the wake of Chuck's huge Kenworth truck.

Captain Holden was waiting anxiously for my arrival. He was afraid that I might have got lost, taking one of the many tracks leading into Saudi Arabia. I told him the story of how I had become stuck in the sand and of Chuck's timely arrival and rescue. He was suitably impressed, realizing the dangers of being stranded in the desert during the heat of the summer months.

After a pleasant lunch and unlimited quantities of cold water to replace the liquid I had lost as perspiration while standing in the open sunlight of the desert, I began my inspection by touring the installation.

The Getty Oil Company facility at Mina Saoud was a complete surprise to me. I had assumed that it would comprise a modern facility; well to the forefront of technology. This was not the case at all. The accommodation and offices were either dilapidated prefabricated units, or old trailers that had seen better days. The former were used as laboratories and offices, while the latter comprised the staff accommodation.

The utilities and process plant stood unprotected in the open air. It was rusty and unpainted. The single seawater evaporator that provided the drinking water for the camp was old and badly corroded. It was a genuine heirloom! Initially it had seen service on a battleship during the First World War. Later it had been rescued from the breaker's yard by the Kuwait Oil Company who required an evaporator for their initial start-up period in Kuwait. When the permanent evaporators were finally installed at the KOC Power and Water Plant at Mina Al-Ahmedi, the temporary evaporator was removed and placed in the scrap yard.

Paul Getty learnt of its existence and borrowed it from the Kuwait Oil Company for the mobilization of his operation in the neutral zone. However, in this case the unit became a permanent part of the Getty installation.

The engineer showing me around was quite embarrassed. He apologized profusely for the various bandages, pads and wires that seemed to strap and hold the evaporator together. He explained that because the metal of the evaporator was so thin, due to age and corrosion, it was no longer possible to repair the pipes and vessels by welding. The welding arc, instead of sealing the holes and leakes, would burn larger holes in the paper-thin metal.

Consequently, whenever a leak developed, the maintenance staff had to plug the leakage with tape, rubber pads or plastic materials. It must have been quite painful for the engineer, who was obviously a dedicated professional, to admit to this!

I completed my survey, taking all necessary notes for my report and promised Captain Holden that I would have it ready for his perusal as soon as possible. I then departed for home in my car, the front bumper rattling away in the boot, reminding me that the car would have to go into the garage the following day for repairs.

As promised, I prepared the report in the shortest possible time. My calculations indicated that by installing a large steam turbine and boiler at Mina Saoud, in conjunction with a large sea water distillation unit, it would be possible to generate sufficient power and water to supply both Wafra and the Mina Saoud installations to meet all their present and future requirements. The water would be pumped the thirty-six miles to Wafra through an old disused oil line. A rather expensive power line would have to be laid between the two sites, but calculations showed that the whole project would have been paid for in the savings of one year's cost of trucking water from Kuwait City.

I was quite thrilled with my findings, as was Captain Holden when he received the report. He sent me a most complimentary letter thanking me for my help and informing me that he would now forward my report to Mr Getty, who would no doubt show his appreciation for such a detailed and innovative report, which would save the company so much financially.

I heard nothing further about the report for some considerable time, until one day, when I was having dinner with Captain Holden, I remembered it and asked him what had happened about it, assuming that there was the usual delay between approval and implementation, known locally as the 'Saudi Arabian Factor'. Captain Holden coughed nervously looking most embarrassed and then steeling himself for the unpleasant news he had to impart, said, 'I'll show you Mr Getty's letter!' After some searching through the papers on his desk he produced the document which was succinct and to the point.

It was from Paul Getty personally, marked private and confidential. It said, 'Dear Holden, you are in Saudi Arabia to extract and ship crude oil. You are not there to create a water bonanza for the Arabs. Please inform Tom to this effect!' Needless to say I was quite deflated by this response to what I had believed to be the momentous business break through of the century. The savings it offered to Paul Getty were tremendous to say the least. And he had turned it down simply because he did not want to invest capital in Arabia!

Some years later when I was living in Jeddah, Saudi Arabia, I leant that he had finally been forced to implement my recommendations and had proceeded with the project almost exactly as I had recommended. He still managed to save money on the deal! I never received my fee!

Shortly after our meeting, Captain Holden's health failed and he was forced to return to the UK. He was replaced as manager of the Saudi Arabian company by an American oilman, Mr Klein, who was specifically appointed to oversee the installation of the world's then largest oil storage tank. We became good friends and I made regular visits to Mina Saoud to use their beach at weekends.

One day, I was invited to lunch to celebrate the completion of the huge storage tank. Prior to lunch, we toured the site and watched the final preparations being made to test and then commission the great tank. The hydraulic tests were completed just before we left and the engineer in charge gave instructions to drain the test water from the tank. Obviously wishing to demonstrate their efficiency in the presence of their General Manager, his men rushed forward to open the drain valves on the base of the tank. As we turned to leave, the water began to gush from the tank into the drainage channels that had been provided to drain away the huge volume of water.

Suddenly, there was a cracking sound like distant thunder. Our group spun round as one man, just in time to see the tank collapsing in upon itself, like a crumpled paper bag! In their eagerness to drain the tank, the crew had opened the drain valves without opening the air vent valves on the roof of the tank.

Consequently, as the water rushed from the tank, it drew a vacuum above the water, which in turn pulled the walls of the tank in as the water level fell. Mr Klein almost fainted at the sight of this multi-million dollar investment collapsing in ruins.

My heart went out to the General Manager. The thought of having to tell Paul Getty of the accident would not have been any comfort to him. Needless to say, it was not long afterwards that he was transferred to other duties. Tolerance was not one of Paul Getty's strong points.

15

Jimmy Scott

James Scott was a large, heavily built man from the northeast of England. His appearance was awe inspiring, if not aesthetic. He had a small head set upon a thickly muscled bull neck, muscular arms and heavy shoulders set upon a large chest and even larger waist. These physical attributes, together with his aggressive manner and fiery temper, made him a person to tread carefully around. Even his immediate superiors handled Jimmy with care.

His aggressive attitude was unsettling to say the least. When questioned by Charlie Gale, the Manager of the General Workshop and Jimmy's immediate superior, about a repair job that had been in the workshop for an inordinate time, he replied with undiluted aggression.

Jimmy glared at Charlie from under shaggy brows for some seconds. 'If you want, I'll stick a brush handle in my backside and a propeller on my cap,' he said sarcastically, 'then I can fly around and sweep the floor at the same time!' Having delivered this challenging comment, he turned on his heel and marched out of Charlie Gale's office, leaving the manager speechless.

It was only the fact that he was a superb engineer and could exact the maximum effort from his staff, that prevented the management in the Ministry of Electricity & Water terminating his services after such outbursts. The Chief Engineer and the power station management realized the value of Jimmy to the Ministry and ensured his continued employment. As it was, Charlie Gale loathed him and made life as difficult for Jimmy as possible.

Jimmy was an unusual shape. His waist was much larger than his hips and whenever he became agitated, which was frequently, his stomach would joggle up and down and his trousers would slip down around his hips, in danger of falling off completely. Periodically, he would grab the waistband of his pants and hitch them to a safe position, high up around his ample waist.

Jimmy was a man to be counted. In spite of his somewhat fearsome aspect and aggressive attitude, he had a heart of gold. Always kind and considerate to his men, he would never ask them to do anything that he was not capable of doing himself. Consequently, his staff adored him and gave him complete loyalty.

A dedicated family man, he was devoted to his wife and children. A typical ex-seagoing chief engineer, he was an extremely capable practical engineer, hard working and hard drinking. No matter how badly he felt after a night's drinking, he was never late for work. Neither did he ever shirk his duties as a result of the 'morning after feeling' that he frequently experienced.

Throughout the period of his stay in Kuwait, he was at continuous war with the management. Jimmy's dislike of the establishment was only exceeded by his dislike and contempt for his immediate superior, Charlie Gale, with whom he maintained a running feud.

Jimmy was responsible for the mechanical section of the Electricity Department's main workshop at Shuwaikh. In the early days, before the purpose-built workshop within the power station site was constructed, the mechanical workshop was located in the port area, at the head of the small boat slipway leading into the inner harbour.

The workshop was quite diverse in its activities. It was not only responsible for repairs to all the Electricity Department's equipment, but was also required to carry out repair work for the various sectors of the government, including the Departments of Health, Education, the Ports Authority and the Public Works Department. Also, it carried out work on an *ad hoc* basis for their various contractors and consultants.

As befitted a workshop in such an isolated area, it was extremely well equipped and versatile; fully capable of handling repairs to vehicles, air conditioners, pumps, valves, turbines and diesel generators. Whatever the work, it was all completed with equal efficiency. Jimmy's in-depth knowledge and experience was invaluable to the Department at that time.

Because of the broad coverage of the workshop's scope of responsibility, Jimmy was faced with continuous pressure from all his clients to treat their specific work on a priority basis. It was a most difficult job and would test the patience of a saint, which Jimmy certainly wasn't. No matter how he tried, he could not satisfy everyone. It was really no wonder that he often lost his temper.

Like everyone, Jimmy had his favourites, to whom he was particularly loyal. He also had his personal dislikes. In particular amongst the latter were consultants. They were the bane of Jimmy's life. He

173

deeply resented management of any sort. He reacted aggressively to anyone who spoke with an edge of authority or condescension in their voice. If they were also a consultant, his aggression turned almost to violence. As a practical engineer with few academic qualifications, the implied superiority in the name 'consultant engineer' immediately raised his ire.

One day, after a rather hectic party the previous evening had left his self control more fragile than usual, Jimmy was summoned rather abruptly from his office, where he had been quietly attempting to still his aching head with an ice pack, while waiting for a dose of aspirin to take effect.

He emerged from the office like an enraged bear, to find the resident consulting engineer for power plant projects awaiting him. The consultant engineer was a pleasant, if somewhat pompous, individual. He had no love for Jimmy, having felt the sharp edge of the Scott tongue on a number of previous occasions and felt that the workshop manager was allowed too much freedom in running his section.

It appeared that the consultant had a problem with his car. He was supposed to take his family to the beach that afternoon and required to have the car repaired in time to meet this commitment. As Jimmy stepped into the bright morning sunlight, the consultant could see from the expression on his face that he was not going to get any cooperation from that quarter. He therefore decided that he would need to exert his authority. Taking a firm grip on the situation he told Jimmy in the most positive and decisive manner he could muster what was wrong with the vehicle and instructed him to, 'Get a move on with the repair and have it ready for collection before lunch time!'

At his words and the tone of his voice, Jimmy swelled

up like a huge bullfrog! His complexion turned from rather sickly white to bright purple. His headache forgotten, he snarled back, 'Not today! The shop is full!' He added somewhat untruthfully, 'We are full with emergency work for the power plant. Take your car away and bring it back later in the week. We will see if we can fit it in then.'

'No, it must be done this morning,' said the consultant, 'I need it today.'

Jimmy snorted like a bull before charging. 'It's not possible today. Take it away and bring it back in a few days, or take it into town and have it fixed at one of the local repair shops.'

'I want it done today,' said the engineer, his hackles rising at Jimmy's tone. 'I know you aren't too busy, before I brought the car in I checked your work schedule,' he bluffed desperately. 'If you refuse to cooperate and obey instructions I will report you to Mr Gale and Mr Addison,' he unwisely continued.

'In that case,' Jimmy said, even more incensed by the threat, 'if you don't move it, I will.'

His voice choking with anger, the consultant replied, 'I'll find Mr Gale and report you. Meanwhile the car will remain here! Don't dare to move it until I return with Mr Gale. He will sort things out. No doubt he will be interested to know how you treat your senior engineers!'

This was the last straw as far as Jimmy was concerned. Upon hearing the consultant's ultimatum, he called three of his men over who had been watching the altercation with undisguised amusement. At his insistence, they lined up behind the car. 'Are you going to move it?' he asked the consultant, 'No? OK. Then I will! Push,' he instucted the men.

In unison the men pushed and the car moved slowly

onto the slipway. The car, a large Morris saloon, moved slowly forward, gathering speed as it ran onto the slope of the slipway. It continued on its path, the three men increasing their effort as the speed increased down the slipway towards the calm water of the harbour. The car struck the water and continued its trajectory down the submerged portion of the ramp. Moving slower now, it continued into deeper water until it came to rest with only a section of its roof and the aerial standing free of the water.

The consultant engineer and Jimmy watched fascinated. Jimmy, now his anger was dissipated by the temerity of his action, was filled with remorse. It was completely foreign to his engineering training to treat a fine piece of machinery in such a manner, but it was done and nothing could change the situation.

The consultant engineer was frozen speechless in horror. He could not believe his eyes. The car, his pride and joy, was submerged in the rising tide. Jimmy's audacious decision and the ensuing action of the three employees, had taken place so rapidly that it was all over before he could react. He was still speechless when Jimmy, although badly shaken by the realization of possible dire consequences resulting from his action, recovered first.

Putting a brave face on things, he turned to the consultant, 'There you are,' he said, 'now go and see Charlie Gale!' He marched back into his office and slammed the door behind him.

Naturally, once he had recovered, the consultant engineer made an immediate complaint to the authorities. Mr Addison, the Chief Engineer, called for an investigation into the circumstances leading up to the incident. Much to the disappointment of Charlie Gale, the Chief Engineer supported Jimmy. Although he did not condone the action taken and gave Jimmy a severe ticking off, he felt that it was wrong for contractors and the consultants to give instructions to the government employees.

Jimmy survived the incident, which created a mystique around him. His audacity was secretly admired by less courageous employees and abhorred by the consultants and contractors, who nevertheless treated him with considerable respect. Few dared to upset him. He was certainly not a man to be trifled with. His staff considered him to be a hero, while the other department engineers at his level and below regarded him with something akin to awe.

Certainly, after this incident, the requirement for the workshop to carry out car repairs for contractors' vehicles was considerably reduced.

Jimmy's wife was as small and dainty as he was large and ungainly. Jimmy thought the world of her. She could, and at times did, scold him like a naughty little boy, while he stood docilely by as her words flowed over him. Like Jimmy, she was from the northeast of England, but unlike him, she had a strong geordie accent, which deepened whenever she became excited. At such times, she was quite unintelligible to anyone not familiar with the geordie dialect.

That year, she and Jimmy were returning home for Christmas. As usual she preceded Jimmy by a few days, in order to have the houes ready for the children when they returned from boarding school for their holidays. This particular trip, she carried with her a number of presents and an oriental lamp made from a painted camel's bladder. These lamps were quite fashionable amongst the expatriates at the time. Many people bought them to add to their memorabilia of the Arab world, or as novelty gifts for their relatives and friends at home.

Arriving at Heathrow Airport on the early morning flight from Kuwait, she was stopped by an overzealous customs inspector as she passed through the 'Green' sector. 'What do you have in that parcel, madam?' he said in an authoritative tone.

'It's ma commel blodder lomp,' she said.

'What, madam?' he queried.

'It's ma commel blodder lomp,' she repeated.

'I am sorry, madam,' he said, wondering what he had got himself into. 'I don't understand. Perhaps you could explain in detail, exactly what you have in that parcel, madam.'

Jimmy's wife, though small and demure, had a short temper, as Jimmy had learnt to his cost on numerous occasions. 'It's ma commel blodder lomp. I've told you twice,' she said in exasperation. 'It's a lomp, a commel blodder lomp! A bluddy, painted comel blodder lomp!'

'My God, madam,' the customs inspector said, 'please take it away before I find out what it is!' No doubt the customs official spent many a sleepless night tossing and turning, wondering what awful thing he had allowed into Britain.

Shortly after returning from their Christmas holiday, Jimmy and his wife decided to retire, leaving Kuwait and taking up residence in the UK once more. They bought a filling station in the northeast of England. Sadly, Jimmy did not live long after returning to his beloved Northumbria. He passed away some two years later from cancer.

Charlie Gale continued to manage the workshop and built a sizeable empire for himself as the Electricity Department grew into the Ministry of Electricity and Water. Gradually, his empire grew, absorbing other

178

departments and sections of the Ministry. A later inclusion was the Stores and Supply section. So large did this section become, that there was no longer room for it under the main workshop roof. Consequently, large quantities of stores had to be stockpiled in large open areas around the main workshop buildings.

One such area contained refrigerators, deep freezers and air conditioners. One day, quite inexplicably, this major stockpile of expensive equipment caught fire. Possibly, a piece of broken glass focused the rays of the sun onto some inflammable waste. Whatever the cause, within a short space of time, the tinder dry wooden cases and packing materials were burning away merrily.

The stores supervisor alerted the workshop fire team and called the local fire brigade. In their excitement at being called to a real fire at last, the workshop team reversed their Land Rover fire tender into a parking post. The fire tender mounted the short post and stuck. The post jammed beneath the chassis, holding the rear wheels some six inches off the ground. No matter how they tried, they could not release the vehicle from this predicament.

The local fire brigade arrived within minutes of receiving the call. They were fully equipped with the most modern sophisticated fire fighting equipment, including the latest fire engines and auxiliary tenders carrying their own water supplies, as would be expected in a desert. Immediately, and with great efficiency, this highly trained team of well-equipped fire fighters took the problem in hand. Hoses were run out and connected to the water tenders. The firemen took their positions around the blaze and the Fire Chief gave orders to commence pumping.

The firemen circled the blazing stockpile, playing

their hoses on the worst area of the fire. Within a short time they had the blaze well under control. A few more minutes would have seen the fire extinguished and a major portion of the stock saved. Then an unforeseen incident changed the whole outcome of the fire.

The firemen ringing the burning stockpile of stacked refrigerator cases were playing their hoses on both the flames and the cases that were still not alight, wetting the latter down to prevent them catching fire. Accidentally, one fireman played the jet of water from his hose too high in the air. The jet sprayed over the flames, briefly spraying on a fireman on the far side of the fire and wetting him to the skin!

He immediately retaliated, directing the jet of water from his hose over the burning stack to saturate the fireman on the far side of the fire. Within minutes, the fire was forgotten as rival firemen sprayed each other with the high pressure hoses. The powerful jets bowled men over. They picked themselves up, shrieking with laughter, recovered their hoses from where they had dropped them and reciprocated with almost hysterical glee.

The Fire Chief tried to rally his men back to their forgotten task of putting out the fire, but he was completely ignored. Finally, beaten back by one well directed jet of water, he returned to his car shaking his head in sad frustration. Meanwhile, the fire receiving a new lease of life, burst into flame once more.

The water battle continued, only to finish when the tenders ran dry and the pumps stopped. By this time, the fire had burnt itself out and the large stock of valuable refrigerators and air conditioners had been completely destroyed.

The Fire Chief finally managed to bring some order to his men in their saturated uniforms. They packed up their equipment, climbed aboard their engines and roared back to the fire station, laughing and cheering amongst themselves like children returning from a school picnic.

Charlie Gale and his staff were left to clear up the pile of twisted metal and ashes, which a few hours previously had been a valuable stock of household appliances. After this incident the Electricity Department decided to transfer its own fire tender to the Fire Department. It also commenced a strict training routine for its own volunteer fire team.

16

Deep Sea Divers

In those days, the Kuwait Ports Authority did not employ its own divers. Whenever diving services were required, Matt Cullen, the Assistant Harbour Master, approached the Marine Department of the Kuwait Oil Company for assistance and the loan of equipment and personnel.

Dave Dichter was the Chief Diver of the Kuwait Oil Company at that time. He was a slim, piratical looking man of medium height with a craggy face tanned to the colour of mahogany. He had a large hooked nose and a gold earring in the lobe of one ear. He owned a large African grey parrot, which he kept in a cage at home; rather than on his shoulder as one might have expected.

His piratical appearance belied his pleasant and kindly nature. A staunch Freemason and family man, Dave was always willing to help anyone with a problem, particularly Matt Cullen, a fellow Mason and a good friend.

In 1955, the Shuwaikh Port Authorities decided that it was time they had their own diving department. Politically, it was embarrassing to admit that the main government port had to rely upon the goodwill of the

182

oil company whenever they required the services of a diver to free a ship's propeller, or carry out underwater inspections and repairs.

In order to rectify the problem and establish their position as the premier port in Kuwait, the Port Director opened a requisition for the necessary diving equipment and advertised for diving and support personnel in both the local and foreign press.

Amongst the many replies received was an application from a Mr Les Doe, an Australian deep sea diver, currently working on a marine construction project for the oil company. As he was available locally, he was immediately called for interview at the Shuwaikh Port offices.

His positive manner and confident approach together with his undisputed wide experience in all aspects of deep sea diving, structural maintenance and underwater inspection and repair, made him a likely candidate. He claimed to have worked at all depths in pressure suits and a casual reference that he held the world record for free diving to depths in excess of 160 feet particularly impressed the interviewing panel. It was no doubt the deciding factor in their decision to employ him. The Kuwaiti members of the panel were suitably impressed! Without further delay, he was offered a position as Chief Port Diver.

Once his own job was secured, he commenced building his own empire. He told the panel that it was essential that the port employ two divers as a safety measure should he have an accident or experience a problem while submerged. He recommended strongly that they consider his partner for employment as the second diver of the team.

Les Doe went on to explain that his current diving partner, a Mr Daniel McGrew, another Australian, who was incidentally, the second best diver in the world, was also available for employment and by coincidence was also working with the same contractor as Les Doe.

The Port Authority swallowed the bait! They employed both Les Doe and Dan McGrew at extremely attractive salaries, which made the rest of the port employees, including Matt, green with envy.

The port did not have any diving equipment at the time. Consequently, the two divers could not do any practical work. This did not mean they remained idle. In no time at all, they had established themselves in a suite of offices in the main port building. Once suitably entrenched, they quickly developed a routine which allowed the days to pass pleasantly, without too much stress or effort on their part.

Some six months later the situation was still the same. The order for the new diving equipment had been delayed pending budget approval, and the two World Champion Deep Sea Divers were still resting on their laurels.

Les Doe was not well liked. He was aggressive and inclined to become argumentative after a few drinks. Les was also a heavy gambler and spent a great deal of his time playing poker with the roustabouts and drillers from the oil rigs.

Dan McGrew, on the other hand, was a likeable person. He effected a piratical beard to go with the profession. He dressed well and his appearance was always clean and smart. A good mixer, people liked him, and he was always in demand socially.

Dan was a man of imagination and a spinner of tall tales. Whenever anyone referenced an experience or mentioned an interesting situation, Dan was always able to cap it with a story of his own! Usually, it involved Dan facing and overcoming tremendous odds or great danger. It was not long before he became affectionately known as Dangerous Dan McGrew.

Within the first few days of his arrival in the Shuwaikh Camp, we learnt that he had walked across Australia at the tender age of ten years, and had sailed the world single-handed by the time he was sixteen! In spite of his stories, Dangerous Dan was popular. Few people were taken in with the tales he told, but because of his pleasant nature everyone tolerated and enjoyed his amusing yarns. When challenged and told that he was lying he would just laugh, never taking offence.

This situation continued for almost a year. Then suddenly, Les Doe found himself in serious trouble. On the strength of his generous salary, he had bought costly camera equipment, gold watches and an expensive car. This extravagant lifestyle resulted in him running into quite heavy debt. Unfortunately, to compound the problem, he experienced a run of bad luck with the cards. Heavy gambling with his oil company friends resulted in large losses.

Although he honoured his gambling debts, no doubt in fear of physical violence from the tough oil men should he renege upon his commitments to them, he omitted to pay the various traders to whom he owed money for the expensive watches, clothing and jewellery he had bought from them. One of his creditors, with less patience than the others, complained to the police, and laid a claim against the Ports Authority, his employer. Naturally, this caused a considerable stir in port management circles. As a result, Les Doe was called before a Disciplinary Board of the Ports Authority. The hearing culminated in Les Doe's employment being terminated and he was sent out of the country within twenty-four hours of his dismissal.

Subsequently, Dan McGrew was promoted to the position of Chief Diver with the corresponding adjustment in salary and a larger office. To celebrate, Dan purchased a new Jaguar saloon, a beautiful car, which he proceeded to crash at regular intervals as he returned, slightly the worse for wear, from the various parties, which constituted his extremely active social life.

Dan took to the position of Chief Diver like a duck to water. Within a short time he was exalted to the more select social level of Kuwait expatriate society, where he mixed freely with embassy officials, the directors of government departments, senior managers and directors of local companies. He rapidly became a regular guest at both the Grey McKenzie and embassy social functions.

In those early days, the Grey McKenzie Company Manager carried possibly even greater social weight than the political agent! For a period both the Grey McKenzie Manager and the political agent flew the Union Jack on their cars. As the Grey McKenzie Manager had the larger car, no doubt he considered himself to be the senior of the two!

One day it was noted that the Grey McKenzie car no longer carried the flag! It was with some satisfaction the local British community assumed that there had been a confrontation and the political agent had won the day. Not withstanding the general dislike of the mantle of empire adopted by the Grey McKenzie managers of the time, the Grey McKenzie parties were regarded as major events in the Kuwait social calendar. Invitations to these events were always eagerly sought after by the Kuwait socialites.

Dangerous Dan McGrew could always be found at

these parties surrounded by a group of ladies. Dressed in his white tuxedo and smoking a large cigar, his eyes sparkling and his beard jutting, he would be describing in detail one of his underwater life or death struggles off the Great Barrier Reef with a great white shark, a giant octopus or a giant clam. His stories were always exciting. At the last minute, faced with inevitable destruction, he would escape from impossible odds by the skin of his teeth.

Suddenly, Dan's cosy and well organized world was shattered! The diving equipment ordered by Matt Cullen arrived at the port! Dan's labourers unpacked the various crates, setting up the equipment at strategically prominent positions around the Diving Department's office, enhancing the atmosphere with an air of no nonsense professionalism and leaving no-one in doubt as to the business of the Department.

By coincidence, within a few days of the arrival of the equipment at the Port, one of the local tugboats fouled a cable, which became wrapped around its propeller, immobilizing the tug. Matt Cullen, in his capacity as Assistant Harbour Master, immediately called upon the Diving Department for help. In order to facilitate the operation, Matt planned that the work would commence the following morning at low tide. The diver, Dan, would then be able to reach the propeller while standing on the sea bed.

The following morning, as arranged, Dangerous Dan, together with his *entourage* of diving attendants, arrived on the quay. After a considerable struggle, Dan was finally attired in his new suit and ready to go.

During the dressing operation, Matt and Charles Spetzia, both of whom had previous diving experience, had begun to doubt that Dan had the extensive diving experience that he claimed. Matt asked Dan if he would rather one of them went down in his place, but Dan refused. Although somewhat shaky and sweating profusely, he said that it was his job and he would do it.

Bravely and without the slightest hesitation, he climbed down the ladder of the harbour wall into the eight or nine feet of water remaining at low tide. His feet touched bottom and he started to wade across to the tugboat, which floated with some five or so feet of water under the keel.

Suddenly, over the communications phone linking Dan with the shore, came his voice hoarse with panic, 'I can't breathe!' he gasped, 'The air has stopped!' Charles Spetzia immediately leapt into the water and swam over to Dan to render what assistance he could. At the same time, Matt ordered the diving crew to increase the pressure of Dan's air supply, and to pull him to shore as quickly as possible.

Fortunately, almost as quickly as it occurred, the emergency was over. Charles treading water above Dan adjusted the valves on his helmet. An inrush of air inflated the suit and Dan shot to the surface like a cork. He lay flat across the water like some larger-than-life Michelin Man. When he saw the emergency was over, Charles swam back to the shore pushing Dan before him like a large rubber raft!

As he pushed Dan towards the quay wall, Charles adjusted the outlet valve to provide Dan with a change of air, keeping sufficient buoyancy in the suit to keep him afloat.

The crew pulled Dan onto the quay and removed his suit. He was badly shaken and in shock. Matt had already called for an ambulance and in a short while Dan was wrapped in blankets and on his way to hospital. When the ambulance carrying him left for the hospital, Charles Spetzia dressed himself in the diving suit and completed the job of removing the wire hawser from the propeller of the tug without further incident.

Afterwards, Charles told us that he had found both the air valves on Dan's helmet completely closed. He had immediately opened the inlet valve to provide Dan with air to breathe, but as the outlet valve was still closed the suit had inflated and lifted Dan to the surface. It seemed that Dan had inadvertently closed both valves, cutting off his own air supply.

Both Matt and Charles, each an experienced diver, had serious doubts regarding Dan's ability as a diver. They were in a quandary as to what steps to take next. If they voiced their suspicions officially, Dan might lose his job. If they said nothing and Dan lost his life through inexperience, it would be on their consciences for the remainder of their lives.

Matt finally made up his mind! He decided that the only course open to him, as Assistant Harbour Master, was to wait until Dan was out of the hospital and then voice their suspicions to him. He would inform Dan that he would take the matter up officially with the Port Authorities.

The Chief Medical Officer, Dr McCreadie, kept Dan in hospital for twenty-four hours under observation and then discharged him as completely fit. As soon as he arrived back at the port he was summoned before Matt Cullen to face charges of incompetence. Dan categorically denied any lack of experience. He cited his considerable experience on the Great Barrier Reef with man-eating sharks, giant clams and other monsters of the deep. Matt, however, was not to be sidetracked by Dan's plausible chatter.

Although he believed Dan to be in the wrong, Matt

decided that it was only fair to give him the benefit of the doubt before submitting an official report of the incident. He therefore decided to insist that Dan underwent an independent test to determine his capability as a diver.

Dan was informed that before he could dive again, he must undergo a diving test at the Kuwait Oil Company Diving School. Probably with the idea that he would be able to bluff his way out of this corner, Dan agreed to take the test. He insisted that it was a complete waste of time and money. Hinting darkly that he thought the management of the Port Authority had something better to do with their money than subject their experienced staff to a test of their capabilities, and they would not be pleased when they found that their staff were being evaluated by an outside organization.

He was so convincing that Matt almost decided to waive the test. Fortunately, common sense prevailed and Dave Dichter, the Chief Diver of the Kuwait Oil Company, was approached officially to carry it out without delay.

The morning of the test arrived and Dan reported to the Chief Diver's office at the Diving School by the main pier at Mina Al-Ahmedi, as scheduled. After a cup of coffee with Dave to settle his nerves, Dan was dressed in the diving suit provided for him by the school. Unfortunately, it was a much older suit than the new 'state of the art' suits bought by the Government and the controls were slightly different.

Before the helmet face plate was screwed into place, Dave Dichter briefed him regarding the proposed test procedure. This involved a descent to the bottom of the sixty-foot deep basin, a walk around the sandy bottom, an emergency ascent, then a controlled return to the bottom to meet up with another diver with whom he would carry out a number of joint manoeuvres and finally to return to the surface to be debriefed and questioned on diving theory.

Dan acknowledged Dave's instructions, then descended the ladder into the water. He reached the bottom safely and answered Dave's enquiry over the intercom system saying that all was well and that he would now walk around.

He then began to walk around the sandy bottom of the basin, but after a few steps he stopped and appeared to be adjusting his helmet valves. Knowing how deceptive distance can be under water, Dave picked up the microphone and was about to ask Dan to move over to the left where a number of hand tools had already been placed on the bottom for his use.

Suddenly, just as Dave was about to pass on the instructions to Dan, the sea water of the basin boiled and bubbled. Then with an explosive 'Whoosh!' Dan shot out of the sea like a cork, rising some four or five feet out of the water before falling back to the surface to float like a huge rigid balloon, bobbing slowly on the slight swell entering the harbour from the open sea beyond.

He was immediately pulled to safety, undressed and a doctor called to examine him. Fortunately, he was unhurt. As soon as Dave Dichter saw that he was unharmed, he instigated a detailed examination of the diving suit to check it for faults. There were none!

Apparently, Dan had once again inadvertently closed the outlet valve on his helmet. The rapid build-up in air pressure had inflated his suit and brought him to the surface with such dramatic effect. Fearing for his safety, rather than send Dan down again, Dave insisted that he sit a written examination. Reluctantly, Dan agreed.

Some two or three days later, Matt received the results of the test. As was expected, Dan had failed completely. The report stated that not only had Dan failed to reach the minimum standard required by the oil company for their diving staff, but he had no practical or theoretical knowledge whatever of the diving craft.

Matt called Dan into his office and confronted him with the report. Once Dan saw that the game was up, he was quite philosophical about the situation and freely admitted that he knew nothing at all about diving. He was quite open about everything and was not in the least embarrassed to speak about it. He bore no grudges and did not try to justify himself.

Apparently, Dan had been a deckhand on the diving boat that employed Les Doe. They had become fast friends and Les had offered to find Dan a job with the Kuwait Port Authority. He promised to teach Dan to dive and allow him to gain experience before it was necessary to dive on his own. Unfortunately for Dan, there were no diving suits available when they arrived at the Kuwait Port, and Les Doe had been dismissed before he could teach Dan to dive!

Matt of course had to report the incident to the authorities. Dan was immediately forbidden to dive again. However, rather than admit their mistake in employing him, the authorities decided that they would let him complete the remainder of his contract term. Consequently, Dan remained, nominally as Chief Diver, but off active duty, for a further twelve months. This was much to the annoyance of Charles Spetzia who had to perform as Port Diver when required, in addition to his own duties, and to add further injury, at a considerably lower salary than Dan was being

192

paid.

Dan's social life continued as though nothing had happened. Although everyone was aware of the situation, he was still in demand for parties and social events. His successful trickery, blatant lies and posturing, appeared to lend him stature and glamour. Consequently, he continued to be a regular guest at embassy and other social gatherings.

Being on full salary without an actual job of work to do, he had ample time to visit the beaches and clubs where the ladies gathered for their socials during the relatively cool mornings of the winter months. As a result of these contacts, he was always sure of obtaining sufficient invitations to parties and social events to keep him occupied on most evenings.

Finally Dan's contract came to an end and he left Kuwait with a hero's fanfare. There were numerous farewell parties in his honour and many tears were shed by various ladies who should have known better. It was rumoured that he might be offered another contract, but this never materialized. Although a confidence trickster and social parasite of the first order, his larger-than-life character and pleasant personality were sadly missed by the community. Dan was always a good talking point and a target for gossip by the ladies. His tall stories kept everyone amused. His departure left a void that was hard to fill.

17

The Music Man

John Shipton, Shippy, was a short, dark complexioned man who could easily be taken for an Arab, southern European or gipsy. This impression was heightened by a predilection to wear flashy continental suits, ties and shirts. During the summer months he was never seen without a coat and tie. In winter, whenever the temperature allowed, he would wear his bespoke tailored suits, highly coloured waistcoats, a smart trilby hat and leather gloves.

Always impeccably, if somewhat flashily, dressed, he stood out in a crowd, particularly so in Kuwait where dress tended to be informal: usually confined to an open-necked, short sleeve shirt, shorts and sandals during the heat of summer and a long sleeve shirt, tie and slacks in winter.

Shippy was extremely sensitive about his dark, olive-coloured skin. He was particularly incensed one day at the airport. He was approached for directions by a newly arrived Welsh expatriate. The man thanked him profusely for his help, then, as an afterthought, turned back to him and said rather condescendingly, 'I say, may I compliment you upon your command of English, it's not often one can speak a second language

194

so fluently!' Shippy almost died of apoplexy. 'What do you mean, mate,' he said, his rather high voice almost raised to a squeak with emotion, 'I'm more bloody English than you are!' He rushed off, shaking with fury.

Shippy had been in the Middle East for a long time. He gained his engineering expertise as a Metro-Vickers apprentice at their Trafford Park works in Manchester. Later, he joined the Iranian Oil Company in 1936 and remained in their service until the European staff were sent out of the country by Dr Mosadek, the Prime Minister of Iran, when he nationalized the oil company in 1950. Shippy, who was by then a senior member of the company remained until the last. For a period, he was thrown into an Iranian jail as a suspected British spy. Later he claimed that his immunity to stomach problems, his fluency in Pharsee and his skill at bridge were all direct results of his sojourn in the Iranian prison.

Finally released from the prison, he returned to England with the few remaining expatriate employees of the Iranian Oil Company. The oil production installations in Iran were closed down and remained so, until the Shah returned to power and deposed Dr Mosadek.

The Iranian Oil Company never regained its previous prominence in the oil producing world. The great international oil companies had already turned their attention to the new and more productive fields of Saudi Arabia and Kuwait. Consequently, the Iranian oilfields were no longer of such great importance to the world.

The resulting upsurge in development of the Kuwait infrastructure, the increase in personal wealth of the citizens and the greatly improved standard of living of the average Kuwaiti, caused an unprecedented demand for power and water. The ensuing growth of the oil industry and the development of these utilities created many lucrative positions for expatriate engineers and technicians. They arrived in droves to construct, operate and maintain the oil production facilities, the power generation and water production plants, together with their associated infrastructure.

Subsequently, in 1952, John Shipton, one of the many ex-Iranian Oil Company expatriates recruited by the Kuwait Government in those early years, was employed as the Instrument Workshop Superintendent at the Shuwaikh Power and Distillation Plant. He quickly established himself in the post and became one of the more valuable employees of the Department of Electricity and Water, later to become the Ministry of Electricity and Water.

Shippy was a man of many talents. During the day, he held court in his large office in the prefabricated building that comprised the Instrument Department of the main workshop complex. His hospitality was famous. At some time during the day, the majority of the engineers in their power station and main workshop facility would find their way to his office for a cup of tea and a chat. Shippy, faining meanness, would quip that it was always advisable to visit him on the first of the month when he put a new tea bag in the pot.

A creature of habit, Shippy was an extremely complex soul. He was an introvert and avoided the company of strangers whenever possible, choosing a small number of friends he would divide his attention between to the exclusion of all others. Many times, he would drive up to a friend's house for a routine visit, but should he see that other visitors were there, he would reverse his car and drive away without calling. The

196

following day he would let the particular friend know that he had called, but left when he realized that they had visitors.

He had a fixed roster for visiting his friends. We all had our appointed evenings on which Shippy called for a chat and a cup of tea. Between ourselves we would refer to these nights as 'Shippy's Night'. We tried to make sure that everyone knew what particular evening it was so that visitors would stay away. He would be most offended if we made other arrangements or had friends around on his 'special' evenings. He would sulk for days afterwards.

Extremely shy in his relationships with women, he longed to have a girlfriend or wife, but he could never drive himself to enter into a personal relationship. He admired pretty young girls, but was afraid to approach them. He would lavish gifts upon them, but was never able to strike up a relationship. Consequently, he sublimated his desire for a girlfriend of his own by seeking the company of wives and daughters of friends. Under these circumstances, he could enjoy female company without having to make a commitment or a direct person to person approach to a female.

Highly intelligent and gifted with an inventive, analytical mind, he was always planning or inventing something. In the early 1950s he drew up plans for a video disk, similar in many respects to the current successful CD. Lasers were not available then and an ordinary beam of incoherent light was not capable of recording or recovering sound and pictures. Nevertheless, his idea to sell popular music recordings in conjunction with moving pictures of the artists was a foretaste of things to come.

Amongst his other inventions which came to nothing were cycle tracks fabricated from old tyres that had been ground and reconstituted into interlocking strips, which could be laid quickly and without foundations alongside a road or footpath, and an electric shaver which used a hot wire to burn off the stubble rather than clip it off. Neither invention came to fruition.

He designed and then manufactured in the instrument workshop, a number of innovative surgical instruments for the local surgeons. One of these, a bowel biopsy instrument, was a great success. Shippy never took out a patent on his design and the instrument was marketed on a worldwide basis by one of the doctors. He made a fortune and Shippy received nothing.

In the belief that the existing shorthand symbols left much to be desired, he invented his own personal shorthand script. His notebooks, overflowing with apparently meaningless hieroglyphics, littered his desk. All his personal notes and reports were written in his shorthand. They were always secure from prying eyes.

A gifted musician who had taught himself to play as a child, John Shipton played a number of instruments as well. Often, he would listen to a musical score from a film or on the radio, write it down on a piece of paper and transpose it for the organ, to play later at one of the dances or his after-cinema recitals for his friends.

His great preference was for the Hammond organ. A shy, retiring person with a large inferiority complex, he delighted to play at the various social functions held throughout Kuwait, enjoying the sense of respect and prestige that such service gave him without him having to make direct personal contact with strangers. He even purchased a Volkswagen Microbus specifically to carry his organs from his room in the Shuwaikh Camp to the various functions and dances held each Thursday evening either in the Hubara Club at Ahmedi, or in the Shuwaikh Club in Kuwait.

A gifted and kindly man, he was ready at a moment's notice to play at any function. One had only to ask and Shippy would appear on the night, complete with his Hammond organs, electronic drums and rhythm accompaniment.

When he first arrived in Kuwait, he organized a band to play at the various dances and social functions. The first week tragedy struck! His drummer had a problem starting his car. He opened the bonnet to locate the problem and asked his wife to start the car. She did so and immediately ran over him! He had left the car in gear. Fortunately, he was not badly hurt. He was hospitalized for a few days and was therefore unable to play with the group at their first dance.

Shippy was most upset, rather than feeling sorry for the victim, he acted as though the man had deliberately engineered the accident in order to embarrass the band. The direct personal contact involved and the many problems inherent in managing a group of musicians, proved too much for Shippy. He disbanded the group and purchased his first Hammond organ. From then on, he gave one-man shows. Sometimes, he would be accompanied by Ted Gowan who helped him to set up his electronic equipment and operate the 'sideman', the electronic percussion unit attached to the organ circuitry, which electronically provided the various dance tempos. Ted loved this privileged position and set himself up as Shippy's minder.

Shippy was always available as a babysitter for the young families. In appreciation, they would set out a snack for him. Shippy would arrive with a large bundle of newspapers under his arm, plop down in a chair and snack and read until the parents returned.

199

At one time two of his men, Bill Stewart and John Sutherland, had small families. He was therefore always assured of at least two babysitting appointments per week, where he would be fed and then be able to relax in the comfort of a home to read his papers.

John Shipton lived in bachelor accommodation in the Shuwaikh Camp. His room was crammed full of musical instruments with little or no room to sit or relax. He had fallen heir to my room boy, John, who true to form drank all the liquor stocks he kept for entertaining his guests. Shippy never drank so the room boy had unlimited use of the liquor. Consequently, the standard of service he provided Shippy was less than adequate.

In order to save money for investment, Shippy catered for himself. He ate like a mouse at home, but demonstrated a huge appetite whenever he went out for a meal. His staple diet was apparently baked beans from a tin that he heated on a small electric hotplate in the corner of his bathroom. His half humorous, half sad claim was that he had a three course lunch, burnt beans, hot beans and cold beans, was quite an accurate assessment.

During the Six Day War when bands of militant Palestinian Arabs roamed the streets, it was quite risky to go into the town. The post office was located in the Safat Square, right in the centre of Kuwait City. In order to collect our mail Shippy and I would drive down to the post office, I would sit in the car with the engine running, while Shippy, who at first glance, with his dark skin and continental style of dress, might be mistaken for an Arab, went into the post office to collect the mail. This system worked well. Throughout the few days of the war and the subsequent period of unrest, we never experienced any problem, whereas other people had some traumatic experiences.

Shippy remained in Kuwait until he was forced to retire because of age. Sadly, his investments, made over the years towards his retirement, had either gone wrong as a result of poor financial judgment or, as in a number of cases, due to out and out fraud.

Certain friends that he had helped finance in business, with a view to sharing in the profits when he retired, had embezzled the money and left for pastures new! When he returned to Manchester he found that his investments had evaporated. The greengrocery shops, fish and chip business and newsagency that he had invested his savings in, had all gone. Either sold and his partners gone, or failed. He found himself destitute, jobless and penniless in Manchester, his home town.

Finally, he was driven to seeking support from the National Assistance, a great blow to his pride from which he never recovered. Completely disheartened, he no longer played his music. We offered to provide him with an organ to allow him to play professionally, but he refused. He had simply lost hope. His only remaining pleasure was a weekly bus ride to Piccadilly Station, where he would have breakfast at the twenty-four-hour cafe, before returning home to his small corporation flat provided for him by the Social Services.

Shortly after returning to England, this extremely talented man fell ill with gastric trouble brought on by not eating. He subsequently died from gangrene of the intestines. His funeral was attended by a handful of friends and relatives.

None of the thousands of people he had entertained during the thirty years he had lived and worked in

Kuwait knew, or possibly even cared, about his sad circumstances during his later years and of his ultimate death.

18

The Suez Conflict

I had been in Kuwait two years and my life was
proceeding smoothly and without incident. I had
settled well into the routine of work and the hectic
social life revolving around the beach and the social
clubs in Kuwait and Ahmedi. Since arriving I had
developed many friendships amongst the oil company
personnel and was as welcome in Ahmedi as I was in
Shuwaikh or Sulaibikhat.

One couple in particular, Harry and Cath Woolley
and their two children, Patricia and Ian, were my
closest friends in Kuwait. They were delightful people.
Harry and Cath were noted throughout Ahmedi for
their kindness and the great hospitality they showed to
everyone.

Shortly after my arrival, Ken Foxton, Eric Jenkins
and I had been to a film night at the Hubara Club
outdoor cinema. As we were returning to our car, we
struck up a conversation with a couple walking along
in the same direction. They introduced themselves as
Harry and Cath Woolley and invited us back to their
home for coffee. This was the start of a friendship
which was to last some forty years.

Harry was a maintenance foreman on the oil

production facilities. Before the war he had played professional football for Blackburn Rovers. In 1946 he had come to Kuwait to install the oil production equipment, flow lines and tanks. Harry and Cath lived in a 'Swede', a wooden framed prefabricated house standing on its own in a sizeable garden. The latter was jealously guarded by Pkassim, their cook general, who watered the trees and shrubs as a daily ritual between his other duties.

The Woolleys were generous, uncomplicated people. People they liked were ever welcome in their home, those they didn't, they avoided. But never, in all the time I knew them, were they heard to make an unkind or derogatory remark about anyone.

Through their friendship we were quickly absorbed into the oil company social whirl. We met many nice and interesting people, many of whom are still friends of ours today. Sonnie and Jim Worthington, Doug and Gretta Chapman, Woggie Goodfellow, Les Davis, who later became general manager of the Kuwait Oil Company, were all part of the Woolley's circle of friends.

As a result of this friendship, most of my spare time was spent at Ahmedi, the oil company town, at the theatre, the socials and dances, the cinema or the swimming pool. There is no doubt that my friendship with Harry and Cath Woolley was the icing on the cake as far as my life in Kuwait was concerned. The two years to 1956 slipped quickly and happily by.

Thursday evening, the start of the Kuwait weekend, was dance night at either the KOC Hubara or the Shuwaikh clubs. The evening would commence with a dinner in the Club and then we would dance all night until one o'clock on Friday morning. Then in summer, we would retire to the beach for a midnight swim. The water at that time of year was lukewarm. As the small wavelets broke along the beach they burst into light with a cold luminous fire. As we swam, the phosphorescence outlined our arms and bodies in a cold, blue light that glowed for a moment as we broke the surface and then faded into darkness as the water drained from us; only to return in all its cold brilliance as we entered the water once again.

After an exhilarating swim, we would return to the Woolley's home for an early breakfast. Then, with the sun rising in a great golden sphere over the desert, we would drive home to catch a few hours' sleep before returning to the beach in the late morning.

Lunch would comprise a hot curry in the Shuwaikh mess and then we would retire to our respective rooms for a siesta until it was time for the evening cinema show. Thus did we pass our weekends.

Without warning, a dark shadow that was to change for ever the West's relationship with the Arab world loomed on the horizon. A newsflash on the morning BBC world news informed us that Britain and France, in cooperation with Israel, had launched an attack on Egypt. British and French paratroops were landing in the canal zone and the Israeli forces were advancing across the Sinai Desert. In frustration the Egyptians were scuttling ships in the Suez Canal, rendering it inoperative.

Some months earlier, Gammal Abdul Nasr, the Egyptian President, had nationalized the Suez Canal. It was the muddled intent of the French and British to regain control of it. The collusion with the Israelis was their undoing. It incensed the whole Arab world against them and alienated the United States of America.

Suddenly, the British troops stopped their advance

and took up holding positions along the canal, which had long since been inoperative by the scuttled ships blocking the entrance to the waterway. The American Government had stepped in, expressing their strong disapproval of the whole operation. They literally forced Britain and France to withdraw. The whole abortive operation had been a complete waste of time and left the canal blocked to shipping for many years. It also alienated the Arab world against the British and French, while strengthening Nasr's image as the only Arab leader ever to have withstood the might of the West and gained what, in the Arab eyes, could be interpreted as a major victory.

Had the British and French completed the process and deposed Gammal Abdul Nasr as President of Egypt, they might have succeeded in regaining credibility in the Arab world. The Arab admires nothing so much as strength and success! As it was, John Foster Dulles, the US Foreign Secretary, vigorously opposed the British and French action. He brought pressure to bear on the two allies, forcing them to relinquish the campaign before it reached its ultimate conclusion and deposed President Nasr.

With hindsight, this was a terrible mistake. Had the British and French forces continued the campaign and deposed Nasr as President of Egypt, the Middle East would hardly have been affected. The subsequent uprisings in the Lebanon, Iraq and Libya would probably never have occurred and the politics of the area would have remained relatively stable. Britain would have maintained her prestige in the area and Kuwait would never have been invaded in 1991.

Nasr, an expert tactician and opportunist, seized the opportunity to capitalize upon this obvious weakness on the part of the allies. He began a concentrated campaign of hate directed against the Western alliance countries. At the same time, capitalizing upon his supposed victory over the allies, he extended his influence to the Yemen, Syria and Iraq. The Palestinians regarded him as their saviour and future hope of ousting Israel from their homeland. So popular did he become, that even moderate Arabs were afraid to voice criticism of either him or his methods.

Overnight in Kuwait, notices went up in previously friendly shops that had solicited our business over the years, stating 'Dogs, French and British not served here!' Friendly Arabs were afraid to speak to us. Less friendly Arabs spat in the street as we passed.

A group of British expatriates from the Ministry of Electricity and Water had been taking Arabic lessons. We turned up for class one day and our Palestinian teacher flatly refused to teach us. Affronted, we decided that if this was the case, we did not want to learn Arabic. Nevertheless this attitude on the part of an intelligent man whom we had regarded as a friend, hurt our feelings considerably.

The Kuwaitis themselves were not ill-disposed towards the British, with whom they had enjoyed friendly relations since the beginning of the century. For many reasons, they would have liked to see Nasr removed from power. His dictatorship had plans to remove the feudal rulers, the Sheikhs, from power, then tie the Arab world into a Muslim empire under his leadership. This was obviously a direct threat to the security of the ruling Al-Sabah family in Kuwait, the various Sheikhs controlling the Gulf States and the King of Saudi Arabia. Nasr was so powerful that they dare not stand against him. Consequently, they paid lip service to his policies to prevent trouble from his supporters in their countries, while at the same time donating huge sums of money to Egypt to keep him from turning his attention to them.

Consequently, the Kuwaitis were unable to show their true feelings. Outnumbered by the expatriate Arabs living in Kuwait, the true Kuwaitis were forced to bend to the will and opinions of the foreign Arabs in their country. In 1956 there were only some 250,000 born and bred Kuwaitis in Kuwait, while there were over 150,000 Palestinian Arabs living there, as either expatriate employees or as naturalized Kuwaitis.

The Palestinian sector formed a powerful political lobby. Yasser Arafat himself lived in Kuwait at that time, working as a draughtsman in the Public Works Department. After the Suez War, he moved into politics and the militant Palestinian movement. With no loyalty to Kuwait, even though many of them had sought and been granted Kuwaiti nationality, their laudable aim was to regain control of their homeland and drive out the foreign Jews who had usurped their lands and homes. Frustrated and angry, they had no country of their own, neither had they the means to recapture Palestine and drive out the Jews as they wished.

Triggered by Nasr's inflammatory speeches, their anger and frustration boiled over. Focusing upon the British, who they blamed for the creation of Israel, they became militant. The Palestine Liberation Organization and many smaller pressure groups of varying degrees of extremism were formed. They believed, with some truth, that the Balfour Declaration had opened the door to the events which had led to the end of the British mandate and the flooding of Palestine by Jewish settlers in 1948. They saw Gammel Abdul Nasr as their champion, a leader who would fight and conquer the Israeli invaders of their homeland. The fact that the conjoined might of Britain, France and Israel had not managed to topple Nasr from power leant considerable credence to their belief that at long last, an invincible champion had arisen to lead them to victory and return their homeland to them.

Wisely, the Kuwaiti authorities tried to contain the problem. British personnel whose presence was not essential at work, were required to stay at home. They were advised to stay away from the *soukh* and centre of the town at night. Consequently, there were a few incidents. One that could have developed into a serious situation occurred when a crowd of dissidents marched on the British Embassy, this was too much for the Kuwaiti authorities to tolerate. Abu Jazzar, Sheikh Nasr, the Governor of Kuwait, suddenly appeared before them, placing his not inconsiderable bulk between them and the Embassy gate, ordering them to disperse. They refused and when they continued to advance, Sheikh Nasr pulled out his pistol and shot one of the more belligerent ring leaders. Faced with this unexpected show of force, the others dispersed peacefully enough.

This incident led the Kuwaiti authorities to take some firmer action. Armed road blocks were set up on the roads leading to and from Kuwait City to check the comings and goings of the citizens. The airport was heavily guarded by the army, as were the major oil installations.

The Kuwait army was staffed by mercenaries, mainly Palestinians and Iraqis. The Al-Sabah family, not trusting these foreign Arab mercenaries, brought in their own tribesmen from the desert. The bedouins were completely loyal to their respective tribal Sheikhs and displayed total contempt for the professional soldiers of the Kuwait Army. They created a flamboyant picture in their flowing robes and *bisht*, with automatic carbines slung over their shoulders, their chests criss-crossed with ammunition bandoliers. They wore cartridge belts and holsters carrying automatic pistols and revolvers around their waists, and always a large, ornamental dagger on prominent display. This together with their completely ruthless loyalty to their Sheikh presented a picture, which promoted either fear or confidence depending upon whether one was for or against their charges.

One morning, we received a call from the power station control room to say that the gas pressure to the boilers had fallen quite drastically. Fred Smith, the Maintenance Engineer, Fred Mackenzie the Deputy Plant Superintendent and myself went out to the gas scrubber and pressure reducing station located five miles away along the Ahmedi Road.

When we arrived at the station we immediately saw that something was wrong. The scrubber unit was tilted over at a crazy angle, leaning against the pressure reducing valve and causing it to malfunction. We climbed out of the car and went over to investigate. At first we thought that the foundations on the scrubber had given way. Then Fred Smith called us over to the pressure reducing valve. 'Someone has been trying to seal off the gland with plasticine!' he said.

Fred Mackenzie, who had served in the navy during the war, said, 'I would put that down if I were you, Fred. It's plastic explosive!' Fred Smith dropped it like a hot cake! Fortunately, it seemed that only one charge had detonated. Had the second charge located on the pressure reducing valve exploded, it would have blown open the main gas line and put the power and desalination plant at Shuwaikh out of commission.

The police were called in and then the army came.

Other installations were inspected and a number of similar devices were discovered on oil flow lines, storage tanks and gas separation plants. It appeared that a group of Egyptian saboteurs had crossed the border into Kuwait from Iraq and set the charges. Fortunately, only one or two of the total charges set actually exploded, doing little damage in the process.

This situation alerted the Kuwaiti authorities to the possibility of further incursions into the country. Guards were increased on all the oil installations and key locations throughout the country. Unfortunately, an over-enthusiastic guard saw one of the Ministry of Electricity and Water's maintenance workers carrying out work at the top of an electricity pylon. Without giving any warning, he took aim and shot the man. After this sad event, it was almost impossible to find anyone willing to work on the overhead lines, in case a trigger-happy bedouin happened to be in the neighbourhood.

In spite of all these problems, life in Kuwait gradually began to return to normal. Other than the inconvenience of not to be served in certain shops, we had no trouble. Rumour had it that gangs of Palestinians roamed the town on the lookout for British and French citizens, but this was never substantiated. In all probability it was pure fabrication designed by the journalists to dramatize the situation.

Some weeks later, were were able to move freely around the city and once again we started visiting the local cinema whenever there was a reasonable film on show.

At that time, there were two local cinemas in Kuwait City, the Al-Firdous and the Al-Hamra. Some years later the Andalous cinema with a Todao wide screen and sound system was constructed, but at the time we had to make do with the two cinemas referenced. The Al-Firdous only showed Arabic and Indian films, but the Al-Hamra screened the latest Western films on a wide screen. We went regularly to see these wide screen epics.

One had to queue at the box office in order to purchase tickets for the evening performance. Shortly after the Suez War, a mandatory tax to assist the Palestinian cause was imposed on all ticket sales. While one waited in the queue to buy tickets, local boy scouts moved up and down the line with collecting boxes. Around their necks they wore a sign in Arabic, while their collection boxes were illustrated with crossed rifles and the new Palestinian flag. Everyone gave them something as a matter of course. There was always deep sympathy for the plight of the homeless refugees, forced by circumstances to live in the camps in the Lebanon and the territories between Israel and Jordan.

It was some weeks later, when out of mild curiosity, I had the notice translated. It read, 'Buy a bullet to kill a Frenchman'. After this none of us contributed to the collection boxes of the innocent looking boy scouts; although we did continue to visit the cinema on a regular basis.

The Al-Hamra cinema was the more modern one of the two. The seating in all the cinemas was divided into two sections, single men's sitting areas and family seating. We always went as a mixed party with Harry and Cath Woolley and another family. As a mixed party we were able to sit in a box on the edge of the balcony, well away from the rows of seats occupied by the single men. Once seated, one tried not to move one's

212

feet too much, because the floor of the boxes were covered with pshtasha nut shells dropped by the previous occupants. The shells crackled and snapped as one's feet moved over them, causing a considerable distraction for people in the adjacent boxes. It was quite usual for a mouse to run alongside the balustrade or across the floor of the box seeking discarded nut kernels or crumbs from the hot-dog and sandwich snacks munched by the audience during the show.

A less attractive aspect of the cinemas was their cockroach population. In the foyer there was a number of fresh juice stands. They comprised a juice-soaked, wooden counter top to which was screwed a hand-operated orange squeezer and a large glass case full of oranges. The drinks were served in tumblers filled from a large jug situated below the squeezer.

When one purchased a drink the operator would slice and squeeze oranges into the jug and then decant the juice into a not too clean-looking tumbler. If one looked closely, the wooden counter top was alive with small insects, which on inspection proved to be young cockroaches. The operator completely ignored their presence as did most of the customers. Prior to the start of the show and during the intervals, these stalls did a roaring trade.

Once inside the cinema, those of us with fore-knowledge would raise our feet well clear of the floor. Otherwise it was almost a certainty that a wandering beetle would climb up one's trouser leg, creating a considerable diversion when discovered. This happened once with John Shipton, an avid cinema-goer. It was a long time before he could be persuaded to visit the cinema again.

On one particular visit to the cinema, to see the epic

Mother India, I saw a large cockroach approaching along the top of the balustrade bordering the balcony. Its size can be appreciated from the fact that I saw it, while some distance away, in the dim light from the cinema screen.

Quite unaware that it had been observed, the gigantic insect trotted blissfully along to meet its ordained fate. As it came level with me, I leant forward and with a powerful flick of my finger, sent it spinning out into space. For a moment its polished shell gleamed in the light from the screen, then it was gone, falling into the depths below.

Almost immediately, from the stalls below, came a loud shout and a thud. Then more shouts. The turmoil apparently coincided with the interval between the reels, because the lights came on and the audience rose to go into the foyer either to relieve themselves or to drink the fresh orange juice served as the refreshment in the lobby.

However, the altercation below continued. I peered cautiously over the balcony to see what the problem was. Below me two Kuwaitis were shouting and slapping at each other with their sandals. By pure chance, my cockroach had fallen directly down the neck of the larger of the two men. For some reason known only to himself, he assumed that his neighbour had dropped it down his neck for a joke. Shouting and slapping each other with their slippers, the men presented quite a sight.

The argument continued unabated, until the cinema attendants arrived on the scene giving the two an ultimatum either to be quiet or leave the cinema. At this threat the argument gradually subsided. Under the direction of the attendants, the men moved grudgingly to alternative seats well away from each other. The attendants stationed themselves against the end of the row of seats to ensure that the two men did not recommence their fight. When the interval ended and the lights dimmed again, peace reigned once more. It was a memorable evening. I was fortunate that the large Kuwaiti had not realized where the cockroach had actually come from.

After the show, the audience left the theatre by exit doors leading to the rear of the building. This procedure segregated them from the crowds waiting at the front of the cinema to see the next show.

As one passed by the rear and side walls of the building, one's nostrils were assailed by the smell of stale urine. Because of the lack of public toilet facilities, the cinema walls were in regular use as urinals by cinema-goers and passers-by alike. The ornamental rendering on the walls was badly stained and corroded by continuous dousing with urine. The corrosive liquid seeped into the concrete, corroding the reinforcing steel, causing great damage to the structure of the buildings.

In those early days the Kuwaiti authorities never considered it necessary to build public toilets. Why spend money on such unnecessary luxury as a public convenience when the desert was there for the use of all? Logical thinking to the bedouins, but not for the town dweller. It took many years before the message sank in and public facilities were provided as a matter of routine. Now, of course, such inconveniences are things of the past and Kuwait is like any other modern city.

19

Kuwaiti Friends

Over the years I developed many long-lasting relationships and friendships with a number of Kuwaitis. The secret of these relationships seemed to be based upon mutual tolerance of each other's customs and values, while avoiding intrusion into individual private lives, unless specifically invited to do so.

At regular intervals, my family and I would be invited by our Kuwaiti friends either to dinner, for an afternoon sail or to a beach party. We in turn would return the invitation after a suitable time lapse. I always made it a point never to intrude on their privacy, or force my company on any of our Arab friends

Shortly after my arrival in Kuwait, I met one particular friend, Mohammed Qabazard, the Director of the Shuwaikh port and a local merchant. He was constructing a new house and required advice regarding treatment of his new swimming pool. Like most people seeking advice on water matters, Mohammed approached the Ministry of Electricity and Water's laboratory and myself for help. Fortunately, I was able to assist him in this and other matters. He was appreciative of the help he received and subsequently we became firm friends.

Mohammed Qabazard had built himself a beautiful home. It was located to the west of the Salwah Gardens, a zoo owned by one of the Sheikhs. Quite conservative by the usual standards of Arab architecture, the house was strikingly well designed. The black and gilt railings set around the house and large garden were copies of the railings at Buckingham Palace in London. The lush gardens were well laid out and cared for. The large open air swimming pool was tiled in expensive mosaic tiles. Nothing but the best equipment was installed and everything about the house and gardens breathed good design and quality.

The interior of the house was sumptuous in the extreme. Handmade oriental carpets covered the floors, expensive antiques and ornaments decorated the rooms and halls. The furniture was expensive, but in excellent taste, unlike the garish Louis XIV designs found in the homes of many wealthy Arabs.

One room in particular, the Persian Room, was outstanding in design and decor. The ceiling comprised hand-painted mosaic tiles. Mohammed had commissioned a group of traditional Iranian artists to design the ceiling. They were brought from Iran at great expense to paint and install the ceiling in the Qabazard's new home. Each tile was individually hand-painted in traditional colours. The completed ceiling comprised a pictorial display of traditional Iranian art, including Darius the Great and his court, hunting and playing the ancient Iranian sport of polo. All these scenes were displayed in the exquisite detail usually reserved for the famous Persian miniatures, painted with a cat's whisker on pieces of ivory.

On the floor of the room was a large Persian carpet. It had been specially commissioned by Mohammed from one of the master carpet makers of Iran. The design of the carpet depicted an exact mirror image of the scenes painted on the ceiling mosaic above it. Each scene on the ceiling tiles was reflected in the carpet below.

Both the ceiling and the carpet were priceless, unique works of art. Mohammed was proud to say that the design was perfect except for one single flaw that had been deliberately included in the design. 'Only God may create perfection.' Therefore by tradition, every design had an imperfection deliberately included to prevent any suggestion of competing with the Creator.

Sadly, during the Iraqi invasion of 1991, the Iraqi soldiers vandalized the house. They lit fires on the carpet and smashed the priceless tiles and works of art that Mohammed had so painstakingly collected. The family fled to Saudi Arabia and then to their home in England, where they stayed until the Iraqi forces were driven out of Kuwait.

Mohammed had died in 1989. Fortunately, he was saved the horror of seeing his lovely home desecrated by the invaders, but it was a heartbreaking experience for Mumtaz, his widow, and the children.

My wife, Edith, took Mohammed's daughter, Ismahan for ballet lessons in the early 1960s. They became firm friends and remain so today. Some time later, Ismahan came to stay with us in England while we were home on leave. Lasting memories for her were fish and chips and the Blackpool Pleasure Beach, both of which she thoroughly enjoyed.

We last saw Ismahan in Kuwait just prior to the invasion. She was then happily married to a Kuwaiti doctor and had a growing family. Mumtaz, Ismahan and the children were at their home in England when the invasion took place, but Mohammed's sons and

Ismahan's husband were in Kuwait. Jassim, the elder son and a leading Kuwaiti architect, stayed in Kuwait for a time, but conditions became so bad under the Iraqi rule that the remaining family and their servants decided to flee to Saudi Arabia.

They made arrangements to cross the desert by little-known tracks familiar to the bedouins. Once they started out there was really no turning back for them. They packed what valuables they could carry and started out in the early hours of the morning. After considerable hardship and with some lucky escapes when they encountered Iraqi patrols, they were finally able to cross the border into Saudi Arabia.

By this time they were destitute, with no money and only a limited supply of fuel in their vehicles. Everything of value had been stripped from them by the Iraqi soldiers that they had encountered *en route* to the border. In the depths of despair Jassim suddenly remembered an Arab he had known at school. He had heard from a friend that this man was currently working in Dahran, in the eastern region of Saudi Arabia. Perhaps he could help them to find shelter and food!

After many phone calls, Jassim was finally able to contact this person. The man told him that unfortunately, at that very moment, he was about to leave for the airport to catch a flight for an extended overseas trip. However, if Jassim and his party would make their way to Dahran and his office, money and air tickets to the UK, for the whole party, would be made available to them. Such generosity from a man who was only an acquaintance is typical of true Arab hospitality!

Jassim and his party made their way to Dahran and true to his word, his contact had left money and air tickets for them. Two days later, they were reunited with Mumtaz and the family at their home in Wonersh.

Back to happier days! Mohammed and his sons were keen amateur sailors and scuba divers. Like most wealthy Kuwaiti merchants, the Qabazards owned a large yacht. In Mohammed's case, it was a converted fifteen metre dhow. The boat was capable of a surprisingly high turn of speed. It could show a clean pair of heels to the majority of craft in the Gulf; including the various naval patrol boats, whose business it was to pursue and capture the gold smugglers who plied their trade between the Emirates and India. The smugglers were particularly active throughout the Gulf and Indian Ocean during the fifties and early sixties. Even today, the trade still continues, although on a much reduced scale.

Mohammed was the local agent for the Mercedes marine engines as well as being the Port Director. It is not surprising that his boat would have the most powerful and up-to-date engines available. The craft was fitted with twin Mercedes Benz marine diesel engines. These powerful propulsion units drove the unwieldly looking craft at unbelievable speed across the smooth waters of the Gulf.

The lines of the boat were typical of the locally made craft. The traditional designs had developed over the centuries to meet the conditions of the Gulf. Without the flowing lines of the modern yacht, these boats still had a grace and elegance of their own. Fast and stable in the wave conditions in the Gulf waters, the boat was fitted out to meet every requirement of the owner. Mohammed's boat was no exception. The cabins were well furnished, while on the deck was a large cooking stove used to prepare the afternoon lunches for Mohammed and his guests.

220

Regularly, almost every Friday during the summer period, Mohammed, Mumtaz, their children and a number of close friends, together with a number of servants to care for their needs, would sail out into the Gulf to various small islands and reefs located off the coast of Kuwait. Once there, they would anchor and spend the day eating and dozing in the shade of the deck awning or for the more energetic, swimming and snorkelling. In the late afternoon, they would head back into the setting sun towards Kuwait Port and home again.

On many occasions we would be invited to accompany them. We always looked forward to these pleasant days spent on the clear green waters of the Gulf. We would meet Mohammed and his family at Shuwaikh Port shortly after dawn. Once all the guests were aboard, the *nokadour,* or captain, would cast off and sail eastwards down the deep water channel towards the open sea.

Once out of Kuwait Bay, into the Gulf proper, we would head south, sailing parallel to the coast, until we reahed Mina Saoud located in the neutral zone between Kuwait and Saudi Arabia. At Mina Saoud the *nokadour* would change course again, swinging out to sea and heading eastwards once again. Some four or five miles off the coast we would enter an area of shallow water lying over a series of sand bars and coral reefs.

Here the water was like clear green glass. The sandy bottom and coral outcrops, some twenty feet below the boat, could be clearly seen in great detail. Myriads of small fish swam across the sand and round the coral outcrops. Large hamours, snappers and king fish appeared out of the deeper waters to glide across the white sand, before disappearing into the depths once again. Sometimes a small shark or barracuda was spotted, but these appeared to confine themselves to the deeper water surrounding the reefs. The larger, more dangerous fish seemed to keep clear of these shoals altogether, possibly because of the tidal races which developed as the tide flooded and ebbed across the shallows.

Mohammed instructed the captain to anchor the boat and then he and his sons would leap over the side with their spear guns, intent upon capturing a number of hamour, red snapper or king fish for lunch. The less adventurous amongst us would climb down ladders over the side and swim in the clear, lukewarm water surrounding the boat.

At times the rapid tidal flow over the shallow reef, sometimes in excess of four knots, would tend to pull the less strong swimmers away from the boat. The captain would then have to raise anchor and sail after them before they were drawn into the deeper and more hazardous areas of the Gulf, the haunt of large sharks and barracuda.

On one occasion while swimming around the boat, happy and at peace with the world, something plopped into the water next to me. Turning, I saw that it was a severed fish head. It was immediately followed by other similar objects, including the entrails and guts. The cooks on board were cleaning the fish that Mohammed and his sons had caught earlier for lunch. They were throwing the entrails and offal overboard as they worked.

Immediately the pieces of bloody flesh fell into the water they were surrounded by large numbers of small fish pulling and tearing at the pieces. Being fully aware of the proximity of large sharks in the deeper water surrounding the shoals, I knew it would only be a matter of time before one came along to investigate the appetizing smell of fresh blood that must by then have permeated the water. Quickly, I swam around to the ladder to climb aboard out of any possible danger.

To my horror, my access to the ladder was blocked by a large, elderly Kuwait lady. She stood on the bottom rung of the ladder up to her ample waist in the water. She was fully dressed from head to toe in a black *abbaya* that floated around her in the slight ocean swell. She saw that I wished to leave the water, but she was unable to climb back aboard without assistance from above.

Not quite panicking, but becoming more and more anxious as the minutes ticked by, wild thoughts raced through my mind. Should a shark, attracted by the blood and offal in the water, swim by, it might well be unable to resist a pair of beefy legs dangling by its nose. They would be difficult to miss in the crystal clear water!

The thought was not pleasant. Quite coldly and calculatingly, I found myself working out a desperate plan. Should a shark appear near the boat, I would, without hesitation, climb over this elderly lady to safety. Then, as a sop to my conscience, if it was not too late and the shark hadn't taken advantage of her helplessness as she floated half in and half out of the water, I would pull her up onto the deck out of harm's way.

Not particularly gentlemanly thoughts, I admit, but one feels extremely vulnerable when one's legs are dangling in twenty feet of potentially shark infested water. At such times the niceties of good manners and chivalry tend to disappear.

Then there was a shout from the deck telling us that lunch was about to be served. Willing hands pulled the elderly lady aboard and I quickly followed her up the now vacant ladder.

None too soon, I might add! No sooner was I aboard, than a dark fin broke the surface of the sea and one of the severed fish heads disappeared in a swirl of water. A large shark, at least three metres in length, circled the boat, lazily picking up the pieces of offal floating on the surface. When all had been eaten, it circled the boat a couple of times and then vanished as quickly as it had appeared, leaving the crystal clear water looking as innocent and inviting as before. Needless to say, neither I nor any of the guests swam from the boat again that day, or for some time afterwards. The presence of the shark did not deter Mohammed or his sons. Immediately after lunch they went back into the water with their spear guns after more game.

Lunch was an idyllic affair. Ravenously hungry by this time, the party attacked the dishes that Mohammed's two cooks and helpers had provided. Curry and rice, grilled fresh fish caught by Mohammed and his sons, roast lamb stuffed with rice and chicken, all followed by a selection of sweets and fruit.

Replete, we lay down on towels placed on the deck to doze away the afternoon. The *nokadour* hauled up the anchor and started the engine, cruising slowly into the wind to provide a cooling breeze for us.

We roused once more in the late afternoon, to drink sweet mint tea and finish off the remaining sweets and fruit. Then at a word from Mohammed, the *nokadour* swung the boat around and headed back towards Kuwait and the Shuwaikh Port once again. Hot and tired, the party waited eagerly for the boat to dock.

Once back on firm ground we said our *salaams* to Mohammed and his family, then climbed into our cars to rush home, tired, sunburnt and dehydrated, ready to luxuriate in a cold shower. Then, after dressing in clean clothes once more, to relax in an easy chair with a good book while sipping numerous long, cool drinks to replace the water lost during the day.

We had many other Kuwaiti friends. Colonel Essa Sharb was in charge of the special police. A fun-loving and pleasant man, he had been trained at Hendon Police College in the UK. He had a strongly developed English sense of humour and always had a joke or amusing story to tell.

Essa was a great friend of Harry and Ruby McNeice from Ulster. Harry was the local Postmaster General. Harry and Ruby had two young children and one day Ruby caught the little boy playing with himself in the bath. She scolded him about it, but unperturbed he said, 'Dinna worry, it's growing on me not on you!' This tickled Essa's sense of humour and he delighted to tell the story.

Mohammed Faraj was another good friend with a sense of humour. His father had been a friend of Captain Shakespeare who was involved in negotiating the oil concessions for Britain. Interestingly, he had a number of Captain Shakespeare's original letters concerning the negotiations for the oil rights.

Mohammed usually wore western dress, but every now and then he would appear in my office in his Kuwaiti garb. He laughingly referred to it as his 'milking suit'. Whenever he wanted a favour from someone or wished to exert pressure upon a foreigner, he would wear his Arab robes. He always seemed to get what he wanted, so the ploy must have worked.

The presence of so many good friends, both expatriate and local, made life in those early days a delight.

Abbas Salim Shatti, one of the most honest and truly

religious men that I have ever known, worked for me in the laboratory in the early years. He was tolerant and generous towards all. The recent trend to Muslim fundamentalism was completely foreign to his understanding of religion.

Initially Abbas worked in the laboratory as foreman of the chemical dosing team. Unlike most Kuwaitis who prefer to work in commerce, Abbas had no objection to doing hard physical work. We became firm friends and I was able to help him start a business in the chemical service field. It prospered and finally Abbas was able to leave his job with the Ministry and work full time in his new business. Over the years he prospered and he became a wealthy and successful businessman, but in spite of his success, he remained as uncomplicated and honest as he was when I first met him, some forty years ago.

20

Lost Friends

Life as an expatriate was so full of activity and interest that one never thought of sickness or death. Not seriously that is. Although from time to time, when one was the recipient of a dose of the 'squitters' as 'tummy trouble' was inelegantly known, one felt that one was about to die, or even sometimes wished that one could die!

Nevertheless, the odd fatalities amongst the expatriate community did occur. These were sad days for all, because of the close personal contact the expatriates had in those days. The few deaths that did occur were usually due to road accidents amongst the contractors. It was on rare occasions that one of the permanent employees died.

My first contact with death overseas was an extremely sad case. The Government had recently banned the use of alcohol. Not to be beaten, the expatriate community started making their own wines from grape juice and a potent liquor called 'flash', by distilling a fermented mixture of sugar, rice and sometimes even ripe dates. This distillate was a potent, but innocuous looking, water-white, uncut spirit, well over 100 per cent proof.

All the hardened drinkers consumed this liquor in huge quantities. Many became so dependent upon it that they even carried flasks of it with them when they went back to the UK on leave.

One day a certain lady went to clean her son's flat in readiness for his return from his annual leave. When she finshed her chores, she sat down and made herself a gin and tonic, or rather a flash and tonic from a bottle of alcohol she had found in a cupboard in the flat. She finished her drink and went home.

The following morning she rose as usual and sent her husband off to work. Some two hours later the matron at the hospital received a strange phone call. 'Help me, please! I have gone blind,' said a familiar feminine voice that she couldn't quite place. She asked who was calling, but the phone had gone dead. The matron immediately called out an ambulance and toured round the expatriate married quarters, checking on all the ladies she knew. Finally, she arrived at the last house in the line and as she recalled who lived there, she recognized the voice she had heard over the phone.

Receiving no reply to her knock and fearing the worst, she broke into the house with the help of the ambulance men. They found the lady of the house lying on the floor in a coma, the telephone still off the hook.

They rushed her to the hospital, but they could do nothing to save her. The bottle of water-white alcohol she had used to make her relaxing flash and tonic of the previous day was not flash at all, but concentrated methyl alcohol that her son used in his go-kart.

Methyl alcohol is extremely poisonous material. If imbibed, it destroys the nervous system over a period of twenty-four hours. Once ingested, there is little hope of recovery, even in that remote possibility, the victim is usually left blinded and partially paralyzed.

Peter Wilson, the doctor handling the case, was kindness itself. He made every possible effort to save the family distress and under his influence the body was released for burial within days, without the long, drawn out enquiries that usually took place under such circumstances.

Naturally, the victim's husband was totally distraught. He was completely incapable of doing anything in regard to making the funeral arrangements. This was left to his friends and the community in general, who had all rallied round to help. On the day of the funeral, he had to be supported throughout the service and the burial, otherwise he would have collapsed.

There were no Christian undertakers in Kuwait to prepare the body for burial, or to make arrangements for the funeral. By chance, we found that the Embassy kept a supply of coffins for Christian burials.

Finding the Christian cemetery was more difficult. We finally located it along the Basrah Road, beyond Sulaibikhat. What a terrible, desolate place it was! A low mud wall with a single iron gateway surrounded the place. The rock hard ground was a bare stoney waste. Raised mounds marked the graves, some with crude headstones, others with no markers at all. We arranged with the bedouin watchman to have a grave dug in readiness for the next day.

One of the contractors arranged for a truck to bring the coffin from the Embassy to the hospital on the following morning. John Shipton arranged for the service to be held at the American Mission Church in Kuwait.

Early the following morning, a group of us reported

229

to the hospital and carried the coffin from the waiting truck into the mortuary. I'm not sure now what we expected, but we certainly didn't expect the mortuary attendants to show us the body, which was closely wound in a white cotton sheet and then leave us to it. After some hesitation we picked up the pitiful remains and placed them carefully in the coffin. Then putting the lid in place, we screwed it down, sealing the coffin. There was some delay, as I had to go out to my car to find a screwdriver to tighten the screws. Finally, the job was done and we carried the coffin out to the truck for its journey to the church and then to the cemetery.

The church service was carried out in a sensitive and sympathetic manner and John Shipton's music provided the necessary atmosphere of reverence and solemnity. Once outside in the bright sunlight however, we were back in the harsh world. Once more the coffin was placed in the truck and we followed the cortege to the Christian cemetery for the interrment. We placed the coffin in the grave and the pastor read the final prayers. A few of us remained behind to make sure that the grave would be filled in before nightfall. As we left and those iron gates closed behind us, I looked back and thought what a God-awful place to leave any loved on in.

After this experience, I and a few friends made it our business to organize a committee to improve the cemetery, cleaning it up and planting some shrubs and trees around the area. We organized a fund to pay the gatekeeper to water the plants and keep the graves free of windblown papers and debris.

The Arabs view death in a totally different light to ourselves. When a Muslim dies he should be buried before sunset that same day. His body is washed, either by the family or by women who provide this service. It is then wound in a shroud and placed on a bier which the mourners carry to the graveside. The grave is an 'L' shaped hole in the ground, the foot of the 'L' forming a niche into which the body is placed and the grave is then filled in. Usually, in the case of Sunni Muslims, the grave had no marker of any kind. They believe that once the soul has departed the body is a useless husk, to be disposed of without ceremony or meaning.

The mourning period of three days is a time of prayer and consolation. Each evening, after the *Magreb* prayer, the family receive guests who come to offer condolences. They sit in silence around the head of the family, sharing his grief. Then, after drinking coffee, they tender their *salaams* and depart.

In the latter years of my stay in Kuwait three other friends died. Conditions had not improved and our services were required as before. Each time was unpleasant and traumatic for us.

Shortly before leaving Kuwait to take up a post in Saudi Arabia, the husband of the lady who died under such tragic circumstances wrote. He was returning to Kuwait to have his wife's body disinterred and transported back to England for burial in the family plot. This created a panic amongst his friends, I was certainly glad that I was leaving before his arrival. We knew that if he was indeed serious about returning his wife's body to England, there was no-one, other than his friends, to dig up the coffin and transfer his wife's body to the lead-lined casket mandatory for transporting a body by air. No-one looked forward to this ordeal.

Fortunately for all concerned, local bureaucracy prevailed and prevented his achieving his desire. He was forced to return to the UK, leaving his wife's body undisturbed in Kuwait.

231

Death is a strange and mysterious thing. Many years later, when I was living and working in Saudi Arabia, I was awakened one night, around three o'clock in the morning, by a most disturbing and vivid dream. I dreamt that my mother was crying and no matter how I tried, I could not comfort her. Shrugging it off as a bad dream, I dropped off to sleep again, but was awakened again some thirty minutes later by exactly the same dream.

It was so vivid that I went downstairs and made myself a cup of tea before returning to bed, but so was the dream in my mind that I could not sleep for the rest of the night. Unlike most dreams that fade with the morning, this one stayed with me and I remembered every detail.

Some days later, I received a letter from my wife to say that my mother had suffered a heart attack and died at midnight UK time on the night of my dream. Three o'clock in the morning in Saudi Arabia coincided exactly with the time of my mother's death in England.

21

Saudi Arabia

In early 1969, I received a call from an American company called Conam Services Inc., based in Los Angeles, California. It appeared that they had been awarded a contract to operate all the Government-owned power and desalination plants in the Kingdom of Saudi Arabia. In order to carry out their contractual commitments, they required the services of a reputed expert to lead their activities in the desalination and power field. Hence their interest in me.

I had no intention, at that time, to leave either Kuwait or my position with the Ministry of Electricity and Water. Neither did I intend to discard the lucrative private consulting practice that I had developed over the years since 1956.

In spite of my obvious lack of interest and many rebuffs, they continued to contact me. Finally, in order to discourage the company once and for all and end these unsettling offers, I decided to demand conditions of employment that they could not possibly accept. I sat down and drew up a list.

When they next contacted me by phone, I recited my conditions of acceptance; sure that they would be rejected. Imagine my surprise when the company agreed to all my demands without hesitation. They even agreed to allow me to continue with my present consultancy practice, providing that no conflict of interest should arise with their contract with the Saudi Government! Hoisted by my own petard, I was faced with an offer that I would have been stupid to refuse and the dilemma that perhaps I should have asked for more!

Resigned to accepting their offer, I visited their local office in Jeddah, Saudi Arabia. There I met their resident manager, Maurice Lipp, a tall, shambling man in late middle-age and his wife, Doris. We liked each other from the start and it was their presence more than anything else that persuaded me to accept the position as Vice President.

During the week that I stayed in Jeddah, I met with the client, Prince Mohammed Al-Faisel head of the Saline Water Conversion Office, Adnan Samman his secretary and 'Mr Fixit' and Yousef Al-Akeel, the financial and administration manager. I also learnt the background to the award of the contract to Conam Services. Apparently, His Royal Highness, Prince Mohammed Faisel, the son of King Faisel, had persuaded his father, the King of Saudi Arabia, to purchase the design of a universal evaporator from the Saline Water Department of the Office of the Interior of the US Government.

Initially believing that the payment for the design also included development of the drawings and specification, he was rapidly disillusioned when further payments were required. He was forced to revert to his father for additional funds to finance the implementation of the universal design for flash evaporators at the site of two large desalination plants, which were to be constructed at Jeddah on the Red Sea coast and at Al-Khobar on the Gulf coast.

In order to avoid excessive penalty charges relating to these construction contracts, Prince Mohammed was required to have operating staff available at these sites three months before construction was completed. It would have been most embarrassing for him had he been forced to revert to his father once again for further funding for the programme which had already over-run its budget on a number of occasions.

Robert Powell, nicknamed Moe, of Conam Services, had met with the Prince through the good offices of Sheikh Kamal Adham, the King's brother-in-law, and Conam's sponsor in the Kingdom. Moe Powell agreed to help the Prince by providing the necessary technical support staff for the project with immediate effect and before any formal agreement could be initiated, in return for a verbal commitment to award Conam Services Inc. a five year operating and maintenance contract for the desalination and power plants operated by the Saline Water Conversion Office.

This commitment saved Prince Mohammed and his Saline Water Conversion Office a considerable sum in penalty payments and the Prince from personal embarrassment. As a result, Conam enjoyed an extremely good relationship with His Royal Highness.

Upon my return to Kuwait, I formally accepted Conam's offer and reluctantly tendered my resignation to the Ministry of Electricity and Water. After seventeen extremely happy years of service, this was harder to do than I had imagined. The then Chief Engineer and good friend, Dr Zaki Abu Eid, tried his best to persuade me to stay on, but by this time my mind was made up.

The Ministry couldn't match the conditions and

salary that I had been offered by Conam in Saudi Arabia and I would have been foolish to let sentimentality interfere with my decision. Therefore, it was with a mixture of sadness and eagerness to tackle a new challenge, thta I said goodbye to Kuwait after many happy years residence there.

On my return journey to the UK, for a month's vacation, I had planned to attend a desalination conference organized by the working party for Fresh Water From The Sea of the European Federation of Chemical Engineers. It was to be held over a five day period in Dubrovnik, Yugoslavia. I had initially arranged to travel with the Kuwaiti delegates from the Ministry. Now, although my plans had changed somewhat, I decided to continue with this programme on my way back to the UK. However, instead of returning to Kuwait after my vacation I planned to go out to Saudi Arabia with my family to take up my new post with Conam Services Inc.

Once at the conference, I had arranged to meet Mr Jack White, the Vice Chairman of Automation Industries Inc., the owners of Conam Services Inc., my new employer, and Robert E. Powell, the President of Conam who had travelled from Los Angeles specifically to meet me.

It was not possible to fly to Dubrovnik directly from Kuwait. We had to fly to Athens to catch a connecting flight. After a pleasant flight we landed in Athens and disembarked. Upon checking with the airline, we found that they had no information concerning our onward flight from Athens. Apparently, the Kuwait travel agent had forgotten to confirm our reservations on the second leg of the journey. The flight to Dubrovnik was over-booked; we were stranded in Athens.

We sat in the transit lounge for a good hour, bemoaning our fate and wondering when we would be able to leave. Suddenly, there was a commotion at the entrance and a party of armed soldiers entered, forcing their way through the crowded lounge. Their commanding officer spoke with the receptionist who pointed towards us. At a word of commend, the party moved over to us. They encircled us with their guns at the ready as their commander approached us, his hand on the butt of an automatic pistol jutting from a holster on his hip.

The officer spoke in excellent English, 'You are Arabs from Kuwait?' One of our party nodded, before I could explain that although with the Kuwaiti party, I was British. The officer nodded and said, 'The Palestinian Arabs have just blown up three hijacked aircraft in Jordan and are holding the passengers and crew hostage. We do not tolerate terrorists here in Greece. Surrender your passports and tickets to the sergeant and remain here until further notice.' Protest as I may, I was still included in the group and they took my passport and ticket along with the rest.

We sat there for a couple of hours, wondering what our fate was going to be. It was not a pleasant situation at all, to be accused of being a terrorist, placed under armed guard in a foreign land without passport, ticket or luggage. Whenever we tried to find someone to help us, the armed guards pushed us back into our seats.

The officer reappeared. 'We do not tolerate terrorists here in Greece,' he repeated, 'your luggage is already on a plane and you will leave at once.' He handed our passports and tickets back to us and ordered his men to escort us out of the lounge onto the tarmac. We were marched over to a waiting Boeing 737 and lined up like criminals at the foot of the boarding steps. The sergeant

237

handed each of us a boarding pass for the aircraft. It is difficult to describe the degree of comfort this single piece of card generated.

The officer walked in front of us as though we were on inspection parade, then had his final say, 'You should not return here,' he almost spat the words at us. 'We don't want you here in Athens.' He stepped back and at a sign from him the guard stepped to one side and we were allowed to climb the steps and enter the aircraft. With intense relief we passed through the doorway into the cabin under the curious scrutiny of the passengers. Our anxieties were finally allayed when we learnt from the officer's conversation with the purser that we were being sent on to Dubrovnik!

The plane, the one we had originally hoped to be aboard, had been about to leave, the passengers had been on board for the best part of three hours awaiting a decision by the authorities whether or not to keep our party in Athens or to send us on our way.

Directed to an empty seat, I found myself sitting next to a lady who appeared to be sobbing quietly into her handkershief. She seemed quite upset at having to leave. Obviously, she must be leaving some loved ones behind, perhaps relatives that she had been visiting, I conjectured.

The engines started and the plane taxied onto the runway. A short pause, while the pilot checked his controls, then we were gathering speed down the runway. Finally airborne we climbed up into the darkening sky above Athens. We were at last on our way to Dubrovnik.

Once we were safely airborne and the 'No Smoking' and 'Seat Belt' signs had been turned off, I relaxed and looked around. The plane was completely full, we were certainly fortunate to be on board. A loud sob from the lady next to me made me look towards her. She was still crying into her handkerchief, which by this time was a sodden rag. 'What is the matter?' I asked rather awkwardly, 'Is there something I can do?'

'No, no-one can help now,' she said.

'My God,' I thought, 'no wonder she is crying, some close relative has obviously died.' Putting as much sympathy into my voice as possible, I said, 'I'm sorry, you have my deepest sympathy. Have you lost a relative?' I was about to tell her about our recent experience, to take her mind off her sorrow.

She stopped crying for a moment and her eyes flashed angrily, 'No, it's nothing like that.' Then turning to me, she whispered in a strong American accent. 'Do you know, there are some terrorists aboard this plane?'

I bit my lip and I wished that I had never started the conversation. 'No!' I said. 'Surely, that's not possible?' She leaned closer towards me, her voice dropping to a conspiratorial whisper.

'Oh, yes! My husband and I are on a touring holiday to the Greek islands, Dubrovnik, Venice and Paris before returning home to New York. We were all ready to leave for Dubrovnik when they told us there would be a delay.

'Later, they said that a group of people had to leave for Dubrovnik on this flight. The stewardess told us that they were terrorists being deported from Greece!

'The plane was fully booked so they took six of our party off to make room for them. Then they put these terrorists, that the Greek Government is deporting, on the flight in their places!' She emitted another great, body racking sob. 'My husband was one of those taken off to make room for them. I don't know when I will see him again. He is back in Athens and I will be in

Dubrovnik! I have never been out of the States on my own before. I may never see him again! He has our tickets and all our money. I don't know what I shall do if he doesn't arrive on the next flight.'

I didn't say anything, just curled up in my seat and pretended to die. The lady ignored my lack of comment and returned to her quiet sobbing, which continued until we landed in Dubrovnik.

I did not see the lady again after we landed. In her state of mind, had she realized that I was partially responsible for her husband's plight, she might have done me some physical harm! The group were scheduled to stay in Dubrovnik for a week, no doubt in that time her husband would have been able to catch up with her again.

I made my way to the hotel where a message was awaiting me from Robert Powell and Jack White. They wished to meet me on the following morning for coffee at the hotel. I phoned their hotel and confirmed the appointment. Then I retired to bed, exhausted, after a hectic, unusual day.

The following morning, bright and early, I went to the conference centre to register and collect my copy of the conference proceedings, tickets for various lunches and the final dinner. The conference was to be held in the old walled city of Dubrovnik. It was an enchanting place. The old buildings and cobbled, traffic-free streets gave one the impression of being transported back into the Middle Ages.

After completing the registration formalities I returned to the hotel to meet with my future employers. I was running a little late, so they were already awaiting me in the hotel lobby. Jack White was a tall, slim, grey-haired gentleman, every inch the corporate executive. Robert Powell introduced himself as Moe Powell. He was thickset and of medium height with the physique of an American football player. He told me later that he had played college football and had been in the US Navy before entering the business world.

I liked them both immediately and I knew that I would enjoy working with them. Jack White was a lawyer by profession and an extremely talented and astute gentleman. In spite of this, he was full of fun and always joking. It did not take me long to realize that he was the brains behind Automation Industries Inc.

Moe Powell was more serious and I was to learn that he was a workaholic visionary, with a single-minded attitude which made his schemes work. When he set his mind on obtaining a project he was usually successful. Jack was the businessman and Moe the entrepreneur.

The hotel they were staying was located some distance from mine near the beach. The beach was separated from the hotel by a plantation of trees. One morning, Jack decided to go for a walk before he went to the conference. He took a well-trodden path through the woods towards the beach. After some minutes he emerged from the trees onto a stretch of fine, golden sand, the calm blue waters of the bay creating an idyllic scene. The beach was quite crowded for so early in the morning. It was some moments before Jack realized that they were all naked. He had stumbled upon one of the nudist beaches which were scattered along the coast of Yugoslavia.

By this time he was well onto the beach and amongst the sunbathers sprawled across the golden sand. Later, he told us that he felt most embarrassed to be standing there fully clothed amongst so many nude people. Without further thought, he took his clothes off and joined them. He swam and chatted with them for some time and then returned to the hotel, where he regaled us with the story of his morning adventure.

The young Kuwaitis were intrigued to say the least. One of them, Samad Hassan, was quite a character. He vowed that he would emulate Jack's tactics the following day. The others, although titillated by the story, were less enthusiastic. They were daunted by the thought of being confronted by so many nude men and women.

The next morning the beach was invaded by the Kuwaiti group, led by Samad Hassan, keen to join in the fun. It was a topic of conversation throughout the conference. I hate to think how many papers and lectures were missed due to the curiosity of the delegates!

The Dubrovnik conference was most successful. Both Jack White and Moe Powell were impressed by the potential for their companies in the desalination and power field.

The remainder of the week passed quite uneventfully. Jack White and Samad Hassan became firm friends. Jack enjoyed Samad's outgoing, confident manner. Had Samad been interested no doubt he could have obtained a good position in Automation Industries. He had other plans however, and some years later became one of the top senior executives in the Kuwait National Petroleum company.

It finally became time for us to go our separate ways. Moe Powell flew out to Saudi Arabia to meet Maurice Lipp and Prince Mohammed. Jack White returned to Los Angeles to report to the Chairman of Automation Industries, Corwin Denny. I left to commence my vacation before leaving for Saudi Arabia with my family.

The late summer weather in England was delightful. All our preparations for departure had been made earlier, our heavy baggage had been sent from Kuwait to Jeddah by road. Nothing now remained but to await our visas and my work permit being issued. Consequently, there were no distractions to prevent us having an enjoyable holiday.

The days passed quickly, each one being fully occupied by day trips to the Lake District, Blackpool and Southport for the children. In the evenings we attended plays, opera and the ballet at theatres in Manchester and Blackpool. It came almost as a shock one morning, when the postman delivered our tickets and copies of our entry visas to Saudi Arabia. The actual visas would be issued at the Jeddah Airport upon our arrival.

Our flight to Jeddah aboard the British Airways VC-10 was pleasant and happily uneventful. Some seven hours after take off we touched down in Jeddah and a new phase of our life abroad began.

As we disembarked we noted the subtle difference in quality between the air of Kuwait and Jeddah. The hot dry air of the desert had given place to a heavy humidity. Moisture condensed upon our skin as we descended onto the tarmac and entered the waiting bus. Even the cold air from the bus's air conditioner felt dank and moist.

Jeddah airport at that time was in the centre of the city. The airport terminal was a single-storey building surrounded by multi-storey buildings which were accommodation for the Hajj pilgrims on their way to Mecca, only eighty miles east of Jeddah.

The immigration and customs hall was without air conditioning and within a short time we were all hot and perspiring. Fortunately we quickly completed the formalities and after collecting our baggage, passed through the glass doors at the end of the customs hall to where Maurice and Doris Lipp were waiting for us. They led us out to their car and drove us to our new home that they had rented for us.

Compared to our flat in Kuwait, the four bedroom villa set in a large walled garden and forecourt that Maurice had rented for us was a palace. My wife Edith and the children loved it. We were met at the door by Qarzi, the cook general, that Maurice had hired for us. He made us welcome and carried our bags upstairs to our rooms. Maurice and Doris then offered to take us to dinner at the Kandara Palace Hotel where they lived at the time. Tired, but hungry, we accepted.

The following morning, being Friday, we had the opportunity to drive around Jeddah. Unlike Kuwait, which by this time was a modern city, Jeddah was full of old buildings and points of interest. It had been the gateway to Mecca for the pilgrims from India and Africa. Even then, the majority of pilgrims arrived by ship. They were housed in huge buildings in the port area until their official guides ferried them by truck and bus up to Mecca.

Eve's tomb, located in a cemetery in the centre of the city, was another historical landmark that struck a chord in one's imagination. The whole area surrounding Jeddah and Mecca was steeped in history, both ancient and modern. Abraham and the Israelites were reputed to have passed through the area on their way to Canaan and the Promised Land. Lawrence of Arabia had lived in Jeddah for a time, as had Philby.

Ninety miles to the east lay the escarpment, part of a range of mountains that rose over five thousand feet above the coastal plain. One of the local contractors, the Bin-Ladin Company, had constructed a road up the escarpment which would not have shamed an alpine pass. A large company by world standards, they

244

were reputed to have the largest fleet of caterpillar equipment in the world next to the United States Army.

It did not take us long to settle in. The house was exactly what we wanted. The large forecourt was ideal for the children and our dog Zarah, a large bull mastiff, to play in. The house boy, Qarzi, and the gardener, Saeed, idolized Zarah. They took great delight in frightening visitors.

Whenever any visitor or guest was about to leave, they would suddenly appear around the corner of the house with Zarah, holding her tightly by the collar. Just before the visitor closed the main gate, they would release the dog. She would tear across the forecourt and throw herself with terrible force at the closing gate. The huge iron gate would shut with a crash and the visitor, white and shaken, would thank God that he had escaped in time.

Qarzi and Saeed would call Zarah and go chuckling back to the kitchen to find a tasty morsel as a reward for their canine friend.

Our children, Tommy aged eight and Elizabeth aged three, rapidly grew to love Jeddah. Even in later years, when they were grown up and working in England, they looked back to their days in Jeddah with great nostalgia.

In many ways the climate was ideal. It never became as hot as Kuwait in the summer and the winters along the Red Sea coast were warm and pleasant. Throughout the year we sailed and swam in the Abhor Creek, ten miles north of Jeddah.

The open sea itself was too dangerous for swimming, along the coastal stretch around Jeddah was a coral reef. The water on the reef varied in depth from a few centimetres to ten or so metres. At the edge of the reef the depth varied from fifty to two hundred metres. Two hundred metres from the edge of the reef, four hundred metres was not unusual. Consequently, deep sea conditions existed right up to the edge of the reef and large predators, shark and barracuda, could frequently be seen swimming up and down along its edge.

Even the Abhor Creek had its unwelcome visitors. Mrs Resacher, the wife of one of our executive officers, used to swim daily across the creek for exercise. One day she happened to glance down through the crystal clear water. A large nine-foot shark was swimming lazily along some ten feet beneath her. She told us that her sprint crawl had never been so good as it was then. She waited on the far side of the creek until someone in a ski boat came within hailing distance and she was able to hitch a ride back across the creek.

22

Sailboats And Ducks

I had not been in Jeddah long before I began to experience problems and frustration, difficulties that one would not imagine to be possible in Kuwait. Communications, people problems, shortage of spare parts, problems with local authorities, all appeared frequently. When one rose in the morning, the problems of the day before were still awaiting a solution and new problems could be expected to arise during the day. One quickly learnt to accept such problems as a matter of course.

Even today, managing and operating a power and desalination plant on the northwest coast of Saudi Arabia on the Red Sea is no easy task. It was particularly difficult in the early 1970s. At that time, communications outside the major centres of Saudi Arabia were virtually non-existent. A telephone call with the outside world had to be booked ten days in advance, and even then the international lines were so poor that many times the connections were broken before business could be completed, or the speech was so garbled that it could not be deciphered.

So difficult was it to secure reliable communications with the outside world, we found it necessary to make a weekly journey from Jeddah to Beirut, where telephone contact was so much better, in order to make overseas calls. Consequently, each week, for over two years, I would commute to Beirut. As regularly as clockwork, every Wednesday morning at 8.00 a.m. I would catch the Middle East Airlines flight from Jeddah to Beirut, where I would check into the Phoenicia Hotel on the Corniche.

After a pleasant lunch on the balcony of the St George's Hotel, watching the sunbathers and water-skiers taking advantage of the St George's Club foreshore and the glorious sunlit sea of St George's Bay, I would retire to my room in the Phoenicia Hotel to commence business: namely making various business phone calls around the world.

In the early part of the afternoon I would telephone my European contacts. Later, before leaving the hotel to return to the airport, I would make my calls to America, in time for the start of business there. Then, with my work for the day completed, I would shower, check out of my room and return to the airport to catch the 7.30 p.m. flight back to Jeddah. These Wednesday excursions were a bright part of the week, an escape from the problems and pressures of the office. When communications improved and it was no longer necessary to go to Beirut, one looked back on these breaks with considerable nostalgia.

Communications within the Kingdom were equally difficult. Phone contact outside the Jeddah, Riyadh and Dammam city limits was almost impossible. Metalled roads only existed between the major towns. Dirt tracks and oiled roads served the other areas.

At the time in question, our company operated two small power and desalination plants, supplying electrical power and drinking water to the coastal towns of

Wedjh and Duba. These two small settlements on the Red Sea coast were located respectively, one hundred and fifty miles and three hundred miles north of the port of Yenbu.

On the outskirts of the town of Wedjh, there was a graded sand airstrip complete with a concrete block control tower and radio shack. Flattered by the title airport, it boasted a daily service by DC-3 aircraft to and from Jeddah. Confirmed reservations on the flight from Jeddah were difficult to obtain. Once at Wedjh, even though the return flight had been booked and reconfirmed weeks in advance, it was extremely unlikely that a seat on a return flight to Jeddah was actually available as scheduled.

On one occasion, when I was fortunate enough to have a seat confirmed on the return flight, I was standing on the dusty airstrip awaiting the arrival of the plane. Suddenly, an old rickety truck drove up in a cloud of dust. The driver and passenger leapt out and began a heated discourse with the airline representative. It seemed that there had been an accident. The grandfather of the driver had been cooking a meal over an open fire, when his *disdasha* or *thobe,* the long cotton gown worn by Arabs, had caught fire. The old man was badly burnt and his grandson wished to send him to hospital in Jeddah for treatment.

Still arguing, the group moved behind the truck. It seemed they had brought the patient with them in readiness for him to catch the plane. The driver lowered the tailgate to expose the badly burnt body of an old man. He was writhing about on a dirty blanket thrown over the hard metal of the pick-up flat bed. Groaning and moaning, the old man was obviously in great pain. Even at a distance it could be seen that he was badly burnt.

249

Completely ignoring the presence of the poor man, the trio continued their bitter argument as to whether he should travel on the plane or not. It appeared the agent would not allow the old man onto the flight in case he died of his burns in transit.

The discourse was interrupted by the arrival of the plane, which landed and then taxied in a cloud of flying dust, coming to a stop in front of the control tower. The passengers disembarked, dispersing into various waiting cars and taxis and the agent returned to the argument with the two relatives.

They had reached an *impasse*. Neither side would give way, then the decision was taken out of their hands. The old man solved the problem for them by dying. Suddenly, he stopped writhing and groaning and lay quietly on the open bed of the truck, free from the terrible pain at last. He had died from his untreated injuries while the three argued.

There was no longer a need for a seat on the plane. The agent returned to his duties. The driver of the truck and his companion started the engine and drove to a far corner of the airfield. There they buried their relative in an area of soft sand, without a marker or any indication to show where the body lay. Life is cheap to the bedouin and death is a certainty they face daily. Fate, Kismet, had decreed that the old man would burn himself and die. *'Allah Karim!'* 'God cares!' So be it, life had to go on.

This sad event brought home to me the fragility of life in the desert and how easily it is to perish from even small injuries. Had the old man been in reach of medical attention he would probably have survived the accident. At the very least, with proper medication he would not have suffered as he did.

Because of the unreliability of the flights, it was

usually necessary to drive the four hundred miles from Jeddah to Wedjh. Our company maintained a regional office, staffed by an Area Supervisor, at the Wedjh Desalination and Power Plant. From this office the Supervisor managed both the Wedjh and the Duba plants. His duties required that he visit the Duba plant two or three times a month. The trip was hazardous as the terrain in the area was rugged and difficult to cross. It took almost eight hours, in a four-wheel drive vehicle to cover the one hundred and fifty miles.

At the time in question, access to the area north of Yenbu could only be made along a rough desert road paralleling the sea; running along the narrow coastal strip between the sea and the mountains. The road clung to a flat rocky coastal plain with the Red Sea to the west and the mountains to the east. To the east, the rugged mountainous terrain of volcanic origin precluded access other than by donkey, camel or four-wheel driven vehicles.

The isolation of the two sites and the complete lack of local amenities made it extremely difficult to obtain and retain the services of qualified, experienced engineers. Few expatriates were willing to accept the loneliness and isolation associated with the position of local supervisor at the Wedjh and Duba facilities. Saudi Arabian engineers totally refused to accept these assignments. They objected strongly to being uprooted from their families and tribal connections in Jeddah and other distant areas. The language barrier was the major stumbling block for the expatriate supervisors. Unable to speak Arabic, they could not join in the community activities at Wedjh and Duba, where strict Muslim standards were maintained and only Arabic was spoken.

Since taking over responsibility for the operation of the Wedjh and Duba plants, we had employed a number of excellent supervisors. Ultimately, each in turn had succumbed to the loneliness and isolation of the area. They had either resigned prematurely before completing their contract, taken to drinking *sadeqi*, the neat alcohol produced in homemade stills from fermented sugar, or had fallen into a moral and physical decline.

In the latter two situations, the company had no option but to withdraw them from the site before they were either arrested for drinking and put into a local Saudi jail for two years, or did themselves or the plant serious harm. One supervisor had succumbed to the pressure of the place and fled the site without even alerting the company. He left the plants in the hands of the local staff without any technical supervision. Fortunately, nothing untoward occurred to draw the client's attention to this deficiency.

At the time in question, the company was facing an extremely difficult situation. The current supervisor at the time, Dallas Rudell, an American, had returned to the United States to be treated for some obscure kidney complaint. Our contract with the Saudi client required that we appoint an immediate replacement to the post, or face contractual penalties. Exposed to this situation the company management was becoming more desperate by the minute to find a permanent solution to the problem.

One morning, at the height of our desperation, there was a knock at the door of the office and a tall, cadaverous looking individual entered. He introduced himself as Herr Reinhardt, an ex-German army officer. We later learnt that he had been an SS officer who had fled to Saudi Arabia to escape arrest by the Allies. He had heard that we were seeking an engineer who would be prepared to live and work at Wedjh or Duba.

I invited him to sit down and have a coffee while we discussed the matter. By this time, we were so desperate to find a site supervisor that I almost locked the door to stop him escaping.

Reinhardt, a qualified engineer with a broad experience in management of projects and plant operation, was a Muslim convert, fluent in both written and spoken Arabic. My first impression of him was that of a technically competent, reserved, introverted person. Being a Muslim he did not drink, an important advantage to a resident of a strict Muslim community. The only apparent relaxation that he allowed himself in his austere life appeared to be sailing. He owned his own boat, a yacht, which was currently moored in the Jeddah Port.

Reinhardt was married with no children. His wife, a well educated Lebanese lady, was prepared to accompany him to Wedjh. As an Arab, she would have no difficulty in integrating into the local community, while his excellent Arabic would allow him to communicate easily with the local Prince and the people of the town. In short, they appeared to be an ideal couple for the job. Long before the interview ended, I had decided to offer him the job of Area Supervisor in charge of both the Wedjh and Duba plants.

Upon being offered the post, Reinhardt requested permission to take his boat to Wedjh. If the company would agree to this concession, he confirmed that both he and his wife would leave immediately for Wedjh. They were prepared to stay there on a permanent basis and would not require the frequent short rest and recuperation periods in Jeddah that we had allowed our previous supervisors. This seemed too good to be true! Not only would it save money for the company, but we would not have the problem of finding a replacement supervisor to cover his absence from the site.

Apparently, a minor licensing problem with the customs people at Jeddah Port prevented Reinhardt taking the yacht with him immediately. Consequently, I agreed to provide him with an additional air ticket to allow him to return to Jeddah to collect the boat, once the problem with the customs authority was resolved. Reinhardt accepted the offer and he and his wife began preparations for their departure to Wedjh.

I should have realized it was all too good to be true, but I was so relieved to find a solution to our problem that I did not 'look the gift horse in the mouth'. Problems, particularly in Saudi Arabia, tend not to be solved so easily. Now somewhat wiser, I have found that whenever things seem to be going well, some problem will raise its ugly head and complicate the situation! His case was no exception.

The first complication to arise involved his work permit and residence visa. Owing to the unusual nature of his residence in Saudi Arabia, based upon the letter from the late King Faisel, Reinhardt was allowed to reside in Saudi Arabia for as long as he wished. To do so, he did not require a conventional residence visa. The letter from the King was on file at the Foreign Ministry. Reinhardt had never completed the formal requirements for a residence permit. Although he had lived in Jeddah since the end of the War, a period of some twenty-five years, he had never formally been recognized as a resident.

Because he did not have a residence permit, he could not obtain a work permit. Everyone told us that with a letter from the King in his possession, obtaining a work permit would not present a problem. At heart, we all believe in the Tooth Fairy!

Unfortunately, although his letter from King Faisel unquestionably allowed him to live in the country, it was not recognized by the Ministry of Foreign Affairs as an official residence permit, so he could not obtain a work permit! Neither would the Ministry denigrate the royal letter by issuing a residence visa. Reinhardt was allowed to live in Saudi Arabia, but was not authorized to work there. Without a work permit a company such as ourselves could not legally employ him. Should we do so, we would be faced with major fines for contravening the labour laws!

As his continued presence at Wedjh was critical to us at that time, we continued to file application after application for his work permit. We had the forlorn hope that some rational official would appreciate the problem and issue a work permit on the strength of the King's letter.

While all this was in process, we received an urgent telex from the local Prince at Wedjh, the plant was shut down, the town was without water and the Plant Supervisor had disappeared. We tried to contact Reinhardt on our two way radio, but to no avail. In desperation, I dispatched my assistant manager, George Sedgewick, by air to investigate the problem, restart the plant and supply water and power once more to the town.

When George arrived at the Wedjh plant the staff informed him that Reinhardt had left for Jeddah ten days previously, leaving the running of the plant in the care of the operating staff. Unfortunately, a minor defect in the diesel generator had caused the plant to shut down. The local staff were unable to restart the plant, resulting in a major water shortage in the village. George corrected the problem with little difficulty and then restarted the plant. Once again water flowed to the village, to the satisfaction of both the Prince and the citizens and to our considerable relief.

As there was no suitable accommodation in the village, George had decided to stay in Reinhardt's house within the confines of the plant compound. When he opened the door of the house with his master key, he was met by a strange, dank, unpleasant odour. The house was filthy dirty. The floor tiles, rugs and carpets were mottled and encrusted with green and yellow stains; even the furniture had not escaped this strange malady.

A slight noise drew George to the bathroom. Cautiously he opened the bathroom door. He fell back in surprise when with a wild flapping of wings, fluttering feathers and a loud indignant quacking, a dozen large ducks half waddled, half flew past him into the house.

Recovering from the shock of his discovery and expecting another surprise at any moment, George advanced cautiously into the bathroom. It was a complete shambles. The bath was full of dirty water and trays of partially eaten, rotting food littered the floor. A thick layer of dark green and yellow excrement covered every horizontal surface. The smell was atrocious and George had to beat a hasty retreat to the relatively fresh air of the house. The ducks had obviously been in residence since Reinhardt and his wife had departed for Jeddah some ten days before!

George called for assistance from the plant operatives and the ducks were finally cornered and chased into an outhouse. He then arranged to have the house cleaned from top to bottom. Although the staff made a thorough job of removing the mess, it was not possible to remove the stains from the furniture, carpets and drapes. They were completely ruined.

In spite of the thorough cleaning, the stale odour that pervaded everything in the house remained. George had hoped to find a bed at 'the house, but the unpleasant odour drove him to desperate measures. He spent the night on a mattress in the plant office. The hard and uncomfortable bed was preferable to the odorous atmosphere of the house and the still visible traces of the ducks' occupancy.

The plant operators informed George that Reinhardt and his wife kept the ducks as family pets. The ducks were permanently quartered in the bathroom and had complete freedom of the house during the day. It seemed that the Reinhardt family lived contentedly, in complete harmony with their ducks and the mess they produced.

Just as George was about to leave for the airport and his return flight to Jeddah, Reinhardt and his wife returned. Reinhardt was full of apologies for causing the company so much embarrassment with the local authorities. Apparently, he had begun to worry about his boat in Jeddah. On the spur of the moment, without informing anyone, he and his wife had flown to Jeddah to try to resolve their difference with the customs people. As one would have expected, they had not been able to solve the problem.

In sheer desperation, Reinhardt and his wife had decided to take the boat without permission and sailed up the coast to Wedjh. It was a stupid thing to do. The customs people knew exactly where he was going and telegraphed ahead. Upon his arrival at Wedjh, the local customs people impounded the boat. Although he could not use it, Reinhardt appeared to be content that

257

his boat was now at Wedjh, almost within sight of his office. He promised George that he would not leave his post again.

George returned to Jeddah to lodge a strong complaint about the state of the house and the ducks. The cumulative effects of George's report, together with the problem of the boat and the fact that we could not obtain a work permit for Reinhardt, necessitated that some drastic action be taken.

The ducks were a major point of concern. The supervisor was supposed to provide accommodation for any of our client's personnel visiting the site. Should they visit the site and have to stay in his 'Duck Sanctuary' we would be open to the most severe criticism.

All our efforts to obtain a work permit for Reinhardt had failed. The authorities were adamant that without a residence visa they could not issue a work permit. The King's letter authorized Reinhardt to live in Saudi Arabia and travel in and out of the country. Protocol prevented them issuing a residence visa over and above the letter of authorization from the King.

Regretfully, we decided to terminate his services with immediate effect. Reinhardt took the decision well and left the Wedjh plant within a few days. The company agreed to ship his personal effects back to Jeddah and promised to supply him with an air ticket to fly back to Wedjh to collect his boat, if and when he managed to sort out the problem with the customs authorities.

Pending the employment of a permanent replacement supervisor, we sent one of our senior operations engineers as a temporary supervisor to the site. Tom Saunders, the engineer, was an ex-Polish resistance fighter who had adopted British nationality after the War. Tom had worked for us in various positions as a troubleshooter, and could be relied upon to operate the plant to the satisfaction of the local community and the Prince.

When Tom arrived in Wedjh his first task was to forward Reinhardt's possessions to Jeddah. This was done with one exception: the ducks! Apparently, the locals had taken advantage of Reinhardt's absence to supplement their diet. The ducks had disappeared completely! The plant operators denied any knowledge of their whereabouts, but Tom was convinced that they had found their way onto the menu of the staff canteen.

Naturally, Reinhardt was extremely upset when he received the news of his pets' disappearance. However, money is a great comforter and he immediately invoiced the company for twelve large ducks.

Having paid Reinhardt for his ducks without protest and presented him with an air ticket to Wedjh as promised, we believed that all our commitments to him had been met. We regretted losing his services, but did not expect to hear from him again.

Tom Saunders was a gregarious man who spoke good Arabic. He settled in rapidly at the site and wasted no time in making friends with the locals. For their amusement, he spun a few yarns about his adventures as a 'Freedom Fighter' in occupied Poland and later in France, where he had been a member of a group sent to assassinate a number of German generals. The locals were suitably impressed.

Some two weeks after his arrival at Wedjh, Tom Saunders was awakened in the early hours of the morning by frenzied knocking. He opened the door to be confronted by an extremely agitated officer of the local militia. 'Mr Tom please help us!' he said in Arabic, 'We are being invaded. The enemy are attacking the port!' The local militia commander had obviously been sufficiently impressed by Tom's stories to warrant asking him for help in their time of need.

The alarm had been sounded by the harbour guard. As he passed Reinhardt's boat, still moored in Wedjh harbour, a splashing noise alongside the hull prompted him to investigate. To his horror and alarm, he saw two black faces rising above the level of the deck, gleaming knives gripped in their teeth.

The local militia were not supplied with ammunition for their weapons. Consequently, discretion appeared to be the better part of valour. Without challenging the intruders, he ran for his life to inform his commanding officer. The Commander, quite convinced that they were under attack, decided to ask the only available foreign military expert, Tom Saunders, for advice.

With a commendable display of courage, Tom, led the small band of militia with their unloaded rifles, down to the harbour. They were followed at a discrete distance by some fifty per cent of the male population of the village who had come along for the excitement. It was Tom's intent to negotiate with the invaders, whoever they were, and hopefully prevent any harm occurring to the residents of the village.

The party arrived at the harbour which seemed to be quiet and tranquil. Cautiously approaching the yacht, they saw two shadowly figures attempting to raise the sails. Unarmed, Tom leapt forward and challenged them. He told them that they were surrounded by the National Guard and ordered them to surrender.

The two figures raised their hands high in the air and turned around. Tom recognized one of them immediately! It was Reinhardt and a friend, complete with blackened faces. They were attempting to hoist the sails prior to sailing the boat out to sea. Reinhardt and his associate surrendered without a struggle and were led away to the local jail by a triumphant, but considerably relieved, group of National Guardsmen.

Apparently, Reinhardt had been unable to resolve the problem with the customs people for the same reason that he could not hold a work permit. He therefore enlisted the help of a friend in a wild scheme to regain possession of his craft. Together they travelled by road to Wedjh, delaying their arrival until after dark. They hid their car on the south side of the harbour and waited until the town was sleeping. After blackening their hands and faces to make themselves less conspicuous, they swam across the harbour, ignoring the possibility that shark and barracuda might be lurking in the dark water.

Their plan was simple. They would climb aboard the boat, cut it loose and drift out to sea on the tide. Once clear of land, they would raise sail and return to Jeddah.

Unfortunately for them, the harbour guard saw them as they climbed onto the yacht. When the guard ran for assistance, they still hoped to escape before he could return with help. Throwing caution to the wind, they attempted to raise sail and cast off before the guard could get back. But Tom's prompt action had thwarted their escape.

If the militia had formally charged Reinhardt and his friend, it is quite likely that they would never have emerged from prison again. However, had the details of the case come to light and it had become known that the National Guard had sought the help of a foreigner to capture two unarmed men, the militia commander would have suffered a major loss of face. Consequently, it is most likely that Reinhardt and his friend would have disappeared into jail and the case would never have come to trial. Nothing further would have been heard of either of them again.

Tom Saunders was well aware of this facet of the situation and went out of his way to help them. He managed to persuade the commanding officer that it would be to his advantage to keep the event low-key. After a considerable amount of discussion, copious quantities of sweet, hot tea and numerous cups of Arabic coffee, the Commander came to a decision acceptable to both parties. Providing they never returned to Wedjh, Reinhardt and his friend could leave, taking their boat with them. They were released and sailed the boat back to Jeddah.

We saw or heard nothing of him for some considerable time. Then, some years later, his name came up again, this time under tragic circumstances. He was then working with a consultant on the Jeddah Islamic Port project. It was alleged that he had been accused of murdering his wife and was being held in prison in Jeddah. The letter from King Faisel once again stood him in good stead! This time it apparently saved him from the executioner's sword.

After this frustrating interlude we decided to compromise in our endeavours to find a suitable area manager for the Wedjh and Duba plants. We engaged a Pakistani supervisor and gave him greater freedom to visit Jeddah for a respite from the pressures and loneliness of Wedjh. This time we were fortunate in our selection of a suitable person and for a number of years we were free from major problems at these sites.

As we settled into life in Jeddah, we found that in many respects it was even more satisfying than life in Kuwait had been. To a transient visitor staying in hotels and faced with the Draconian restrictions placed upon visitors, Saudi Arabia must have seemed like a miserable, austere place to live. But to the established resident, life was full of activities and interests. Our children grew up there and we led a normal family life. Because of the Islamic restrictions we were all subjected to, our social life centred around the home; entertaining and being entertained by friends. This strengthened and enriched family life and cemented more permanent friendships than would be the case in Europe or America, where the pace of life tends to preclude close contact with people.

Some nineteen years later, for business reasons, we moved from Saudi Arabia down to the Sultanate of Oman. As individuals and as a family, we can look back and say that we didn't regret a single day of our stay in either Kuwait, or in Saudi Arabia, and wouldn't change anything should we be given the chance to live our lives over.